KV-190-971

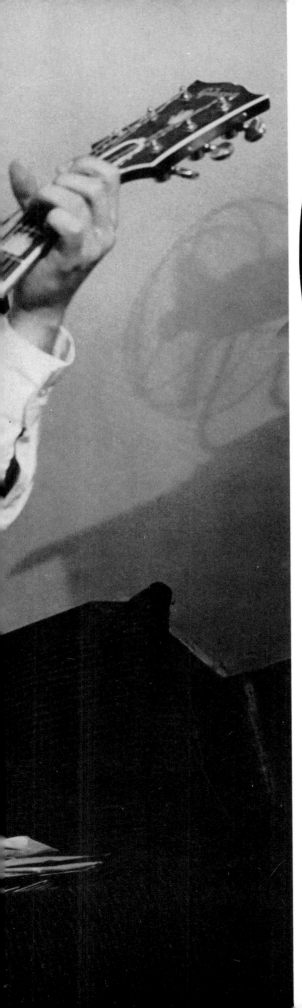

SILVER CLIFF

A 25 YEAR JOURNAL 1958-1983

TONY JASPER

SIDGWICK & JACKSON

LONDON

First published in 1983
by Sidgwick and Jackson Limited
in Great Britain

Copyright © 1983 by Tony Jasper

Design by David Fuller

Picture research by Tony Jasper

ISBN 0-283-98927-0 (softcover)
ISBN 0-283-98928-9 (hardcover)

Typeset by Tellgate Ltd
Printed in Great Britain by
The Garden City Press,
Letchworth, Hertfordshire
for Sidgwick and Jackson Limited
1 Tavistock Chambers
Bloomsbury Way
London WC1A 2SG

AUTHOR'S ACKNOWLEDGEMENTS

Special mention must be made of
Peter Gormley, David Bryce, Di and
Pat of Gormley Management, Janet
Johnson, Harry De Louw, Dezo
Hoffmann, Pat Doncaster, John
Friesen, members of ICRM and
Grapevine, Ruby Pratt.
  And, of course, Cliff.

PHOTO ACKNOWLEDGEMENTS

The author and publishers would
like to thank Dezo Hoffmann for all
his help in supplying illustrations.
All the photographs in this book
were taken by him and were
provided via Rex Features Ltd, with
the exception of those on the
following pages: 123 (BBC); 25, 30-
1, 90, 120-1, 128-9 (EMI); 10, 20
(Eros Films Ltd); 6, 8, 21, 39
(Estudio Quevedo), 104 top, 105,
127 (Tony Jasper's private
collection); 104 bottom, 117 (Janet
Johnson); 70 (3), 71 (3), 72, 91 top
(Hanne Jordan); 125 (Press
Association).

See pages 130-5 for a year-by-year
list of UK record releases.

For Howard and Rosie Mellor
John and Elaine Horner and family
Wendy, Simon, and Rebecca Ellis

Page 1: Taken in Düsseldorf and
displaying an assured and smart-looking
Cliff

Pages 2-3: Palladium Theatre, London.
An unexpected shot of Cliff with guitar

Left: Cherry Wainer is the attractive
lady who is helping Cliff to pack his bags
for the next tour

Year one in the public life of Harry Rodger Webb who became Cliff Richard was eventful. It saw him become a professional singer, sign his first recording contract with EMI, find a manager and agent, have his first record release, appear on television, make a radio debut, tour the UK and form a permanent backing group.

Previous to this he had played in several groups, including The Quintones from his home Cheshunt area and the Dick Teague Skiffle Group. The latter included Terry Smart on drums.

Cliff joined the Skiffle group with some misgivings: 'If there was one thing I didn't dig, it was skiffle, but this seemed a golden chance, so forgetting or at least hiding my dislike of skiffle from Terry who had asked me to audition I said I'd love to have a bash.'

Dick Teague was pleased with Cliff's vocals but somewhat surprised when an embarrassed Cliff said he had neither a guitar nor any guitar-playing know-how. Terry gave him a guitar. It cost five guineas. And Cliff soon learnt the three basic chords G, C, and D7 and practised the popular 'Prisoner's Song' day after day.

Group membership was useful since it gave Cliff experience out front with an audience. Bookings varied from clubs to private functions.

Cliff and Terry soon had ideas of forming their own group to play the rock 'n' roll music they liked and in 1956 they did so, along with a schoolfriend of Cliff's, a rhythm guitarist by the name of Norman Mitham. The trio were to call themselves The Drifters.

They had no money to pay for the hire of a hall or local room for practising so they let loose in the Webbs' house. Council house neighbours did not appreciate the noise and at least one complaint was made to the local authority who sent round their man. He seemed impressed by the trio's youthful dedication and he suggested a compromise. Practice could continue no later than ten o'clock at night and whatever the weather all windows must remain shut.

The trio had several local bookings, including one at the Five Horseshoes public house, in Hoddesdon, Hertfordshire. Here they were heard

by a fellow teenager called Johnny Foster. Foster saw Cliff as a future star and rather fancied himself as a pop manager. He bustled over and with great eloquence charmed the trio into letting him be their manager-cum-agent. Then he spent the ensuing weeks persuading club owners to book this totally unknown outfit who, according to Foster, had a mind-blowing lead vocalist.

An early booking coup of Foster's was a week at the famous 2 i's in September 1956, a small and cramped coffee bar in London's murky Soho area where Cliff and his mates believed it was all happening. Nothing much happened to them, however; no record company producers, A&R men or record company moguls came running up asking for their signatures but they did meet Ian Samwell. Sammy, as he was known, thought they needed a lead guitarist and told them he was the one. All agreed.

The name Harry Webb was soon discarded for Cliff Richard – the former sounded dreadfully dull for an inspiring rock singer. 'The name-change gave me a problem!' says Cliff. 'Sometimes Mum would forget and ask my sister Donna to shout upstairs and wake Harry. Donna had one easy answer: "Who's Harry?"' The first gig after his name change early in 1958 was set for a dance hall in Ripley, Derbyshire. Now a group name was needed. Cliff believes it was Terry

who thought The Planets was a good name. As it happened, Cliff looked up the word in a dictionary and read out the definition it gave: 'Heavenly bodies, wanderers, drifters.' When he said the third word there was a shout of 'That's it!' So The Drifters were born, with everyone unaware that Stateside there was a famous black soul group of the same name, a fact which would later mean they were known by a different name in America.

Just before the Derbyshire event the group entered an amateur talent show at the Trocadero Theatre, the Elephant and Castle, London, but they had to withdraw because some of their equipment broke down. It meant even greater pressure on the aspiring group as they motored north, but things went better in Ripley than they had dared hope.

Soon another break came their way. They had a booking for a talent contest at the Gaumont Cinema, Shepherds Bush, London, in July and

Sammy persuaded an agent, George Ganjou, to come and hear them. Ganjou was not a rock 'n' roller but he was astute. He thought Cliff had enormous visual appeal – the girls would adore him. Ganjou wanted a tape, so the group recorded two familiar rock 'n' roll cuts, 'Lawdy Miss Clawdy' and 'Great Balls of Fire'. Ganjou made sure that Norrie Paramor, his recording friend at EMI, Columbia, heard the tape. Paramor promptly booked the outfit for a proper recording session.

'There and then he told us he thought he'd like to make a record but that he was going away for a fortnight's holiday and that he'd see us as soon as he got back,' said Cliff. 'Can you imagine what those fourteen days were like? It wasn't so bad during the evenings when we were together, but at night, lying awake wondering if he'd meant it, wondering if he might forget us. Supposing the record wasn't any good? It was awful.'

Above: Cliff's Mum and his two sisters

Opposite: November 1959: a rather pensive Cliff backstage at the Odeon, Lewisham, in south-east London

By the time Mr Paramor summoned the group Cliff thought they would be told it was all off. Cliff was wrong. The EMI producer had a song which he thought would be good for their first record release in August, one entitled 'Schoolboy Crush'. The record's other side would be a song of Ian Samwell's titled 'Move It'.

Also in August Ganjou made a booking for four weeks at Butlin's Camp in Clacton-on-Sea. Originally it was for Cliff and Cliff alone, but when he made a scene it was agreed that he would play with his mates to the summer tourists.

On 9 August 1958 Cliff Richard signed with the Columbia record division of EMI and became a professional, bidding goodbye to Ferguson's, the radio and TV factory where he worked. Here begins Cliff's twenty-five professional years of astounding success, a longevity in the business unequalled by any other British artiste. Later that month his first record, 'Schoolboy Crush', was released.

Radio Luxembourg was first in with airplay for the record, though to the surprise of Cliff and the group they played 'Move It'. It was the right choice. Within days it was picking up sales.

Cliff made his television debut on 13 September 1958 on the ABC TV pop show *Oh Boy!* The producer was a young bespectacled Oxford graduate by the name of Jack Good. He liked Cliff so much he signed him up for a series of programmes.

Good had been producer of the much-loved programme *Six-Five Special*. Later he would move on to *Wham!* and *Boy Meets Girl*, both for the independent television network, and eventually settle in the United States.

In the early 1980s Good spearheaded a stage revival of *Oh Boy!* at London's Astoria theatre. The show also reappeared in a short television run. Good's philosophy in the eighties is the same as that of earlier times. He castigates television producers who see TV pop potential only in current chart material. Good believes producers should get out and film and make their own artistes. In 1958 Cliff was an example of this. It is hard to think of an untried first-record artiste who would be risked on a major television series in British pop television in the 1980s.

Cliff's first UK tour began on 5 October, with The Kalin Twins headlining. Their claim to fame lay in their hit single 'When'. In those days the fact that they were American was enough for them to be presumed to be way ahead of any British artiste. The UK audiences thought otherwise as Cliff and his group outshone them and won a much more enthusiastic response.

Cliff's group now comprised Ian Samwell on bass guitar, Terry Smart on drums and two guys by the name of Hank Marvin and Bruce Welch. Marvin had been at the 2 i's on the September evening when John Foster had gone to the club with thoughts of inviting Tony Sheridan, who played in the early Beatle line-up in Germany, to join them. Sheridan didn't show up. Marvin was there. He agreed to play with Cliff and the others on condition that a mate of his called Bruce Welch could join as well. There were no objections.

Cliff made his radio debut on 25 October on the popular BBC Light Programme morning show *Saturday Club*, which was hosted by Brian Matthew. Naturally the hit single was featured.

Soon film parts for Cliff were being discussed as well as appearances at the major dance halls of the time, for this was still the era when thousands went to dance to live bands.

Within three months of signing with Columbia Cliff's income was running into three figures a week. He found himself a bachelor flat in London's West End and fifteen-year-old sister Donella looked after the running of the place. 'She's very good,' said Cliff about his sister's efforts at clearing up the mess in his flat. He still went home, as often as he could, to see his Mum and Dad.

Cliff also briefly had a new manager, Franklyn Boyd. Foster had taken Cliff as far as he could and handed over to Boyd in late September/early October.

In December Jet Harris joined Cliff's backing group. He had been with Mickie (later a famous producer) and Dave Most (a well-known song publisher) of the Most Brothers on Cliff's UK tour. Sammy left towards the end of the year, having decided to devote his time to songwriting, which he found preferable to the noise and aggression of touring. Terry Smart joined the navy and Tony Meeham became drummer.

Cliff hysteria spread wildly. 'Coming away from a show during one of my tours the kids were so excited that they got a bit out of hand. It was just impossible for me to get away from the theatre. To disperse the crowds the police, to my horror, called out the fire hoses. It was a nightmare scene and made me feel quite sick.' This was 1958 and Britain was calling out for a major male pop star.

Opposite: A jukebox with some of his hits – no wonder he looks pleased

Below: Taken at an *Oh Boy!* TV recording

Below: Toothy grin from Cliff, appearing in *Serious Charge*

Opposite: Cliff with fellow hit-maker Marty Wilde on the *Oh Boy!* set

The year 1959 saw more hit records for Cliff, his first EP disc, and a debut album. He appeared in his first film, *Serious Charge*. He followed this in early autumn with the filming of *Expresso Bongo*. He went overseas for the first time. Another 'first' was in pantomime. And he began to win awards. He also found himself with a new manager when Tito Burns replaced Franklyn Boyd. And in October his backing group became The Shadows.

Valentine, a girls' love magazine of the time, told its readers: 'It's the surest sign of big fame when it is necessary to mention only the star's first name. Elvis, Tommy . . . no need to add a surname to those. And now Cliff.' Cliff, they said, 'loves pink socks and reading in front of an open fire whilst there's a storm outside. He doesn't smoke and simply hates putting on a false smile for photographers.' They said he was tallish, slim, dark-eyed, intense. His hair was described as tousled, as though he had come straight from having a shower. They called him one of the hottest bets in show biz.

The now constant bustle meant Cliff had a problem finding time for himself. Soccer, badminton, tennis and regular swimming with mother and eldest sister Donna became luxuries, but at least success had rewards. He was able to buy himself a fabulous pink and black motor scooter. It was something he had wanted ever since he had seen the scooters owned by Bruce and Hank. It was quickly named The Zombie. 'Up went the L plates and I was off!' Cliff says with a smile. He practised whenever he could around the quiet lanes near his parents' house in Cheshunt. He even drove it from his London flat to concert rehearsals at Finsbury Park's theatre. Along the way was a home for handicapped girls. They soon learnt his time schedules and waved as he passed. They surprised him one afternoon by stopping him and presenting a complete scooter cleaning kit which they had made.

The June 1959 issue of *Hit Parade* told of his continuing love for all aspects of Far Eastern life, especially the food. He named his favourite dish as Madras meat curry, fried rice, pancake rolls and soft noodles. He told of how after finishing a show at the Odeon, Tottenham Court Road, London, he – along with Cherry Wainer, The Dallas Boys, Neville Taylor, Jack Good and some friends – had left London at 11.30 pm and raced down to Brighton to try out a new Chinese restaurant, the Lotus House. They arrived in Brighton at 1.15 am and enjoyed every minute of the meal. He also revealed that he had bought himself a super hi-fi stereo unit from royalties received from 'Move It'. It was a far cry from his first record player which was a wind-up clockwork machine which he had been given as a child in Lucknow, India.

He told Keith Goodwin of the *New Musical Express* that he believed in being sentimental, but only to a degree. He said: 'It can get really out of hand if you don't watch it, especially when it comes to such things as theatre programmes . . . even so I keep all the little souvenirs and charms that my fans send me, for sentimental reasons; also I try and collect all the photos people take of me for my mother's picture album.'

The *NME* ran a special tribute to Cliff's first marvellous year in their issue for the week ending 25 September. Cliff said; 'Sometimes I think it's all a dream.' He named Elvis as the greatest, and of the British singing contingent of the time he said he had the utmost respect for Marty Wilde.

In the same issue Alma Cogan said: 'Cliff's a darling, he's so polite, well brought up and good mannered.' Jayne Mansfield commented: 'I think Cliff Richard's the most!' Many, including Sammy Samwell, took ads and congratulated the one-year-old pop star. He was not quite nineteen.

'I just live for rock 'n' roll,' he said at the time.

It was the *NME* and its readers who gave Cliff his first award when he topped their readers' poll as the Best New Singer in February 1959. Various category awards came Cliff's way regularly from readers of that music weekly.

The constant pressure of Cliff's pop activities had led to the departure of Franklyn Boyd as manager near the end of 1958. In Cliff's early paperback, *It's Great To Be Young*, published in 1960, he commented: 'Franklyn is a music publisher and he's also an entertainer in his own

right. In a way I was just another job to him and what he couldn't have realized at the time he undertook to manage me was the speed with which things were going to happen.'

Cliff said his struggle to fit in all the appointments which came his way was rather like trying to put a difficult jigsaw puzzle together. Newspapers clamoured for interviews, photographers levelled camera lenses at him day in and day out, there were recording sessions, tour rehearsals, future projects for consideration. He badly needed a full-time manager who knew the pop business and who could sort things out.

It was Cherry Wainer who suggested someone called Tito Burns, a former band leader. A meeting was arranged. Agreement was reached and a contract signed in which either side could terminate the arrangement with only three months' notice.

As for the 1959 films, Cliff played a small part in his first one, *Serious Charge*. It starred Anthony Quayle, Sarah Churchill and Andrew Ray. It was an X-certificate film, which hardly pleased under-eighteen-year-old fans who could not see it. Cliff played Curley Thomson, brother of the gang's leader. He sang three numbers – 'Mad', 'No Turning Back' and 'Living Doll'.

Cliff's experience in acting consisted only of some amateur school drama work, but he received a fair amount of praise for his part in *Serious Charge*. Certainly his portrayal of Curley was enough for Val Guest, a British film producer, to offer Cliff a major role in the film to be made of the London stage musical hit of the time, *Expresso Bongo*. He would be cast as Bongo Herbert. Cliff was excited by the *Expresso Bongo* offer. He told *Hit Parade*: 'Certainly I would like to learn all I can. I am naturally excited about this film.'

There were some well-known film names alongside his. One was the star of *Room at the Top*, Laurence Harvey. Harvey would play the part of Bongo Herbert's promoter, a somewhat unscrupulous gentleman by the name of Johnny Jackson who knew how to exploit his young aspiring pop artiste. Cliff's Drifters were to be Bongo's backing group, so there was pleasure all round in the Cliff camp.

For someone as young as nineteen Cliff was astute. He had observed the rise and fall of numerous pop stars and in those early days he had no illusions that he and the others automatically had a long future ahead of them. It was a case of taking things a day, a week, a month at a time. He commented: 'One can never tell how

long rock 'n' roll will last and, frankly, I would like to have some acting experience behind me as well, so that at a moment's notice I could work before film cameras.'

He began filming in early autumn, but he still had hit records and growing fame to keep him occupied as well. The press had decided he was newsworthy and some of their reports sensationalized his activities. There were stories of disturbances at his concerts, mainly caused by jealous boyfriends who objected to the attention Cliff attracted from their girlfriends! 'I can tremble my bottom lip,' said Cliff. 'Did it by accident on television and the girls went mad.'

At London's Lyceum ballroom on 2 February eggs and tomatoes smothered Cliff and his group. Cliff was furious. 'I knew there would be trouble. One boy, who was using filthy language, challenged me to fight. I was so mad I said, "Right, let's go." But the ballroom manager pulled me back.' In another theatre, girls clambered on stage and hung on to him. They kissed and squeezed him and a worried management began to lower the curtains. An angry Cliff ordered the curtains up. He said with passion: 'Hundreds have paid to see the show and they are going to see it.'

His parents worried over reports that he might be physically attacked by warring gangs and distraught lovers. Others screamed that he was sexually obscene; there was one writer who slammed home with: 'His violent hip-swinging was revolting – hardly the kind of performance any parent would wish his children to witness.'

It was just like the early Elvis saga, only this time it was Britain, a country which for too long had been merely the selling ground for American record companies and their artistes. Britain now had a star of its own who was causing commotion. Not everybody was outraged. A Jean Gamble article in *Reveillie* of 30 April was headlined HE DOESN'T TRY TO BE SEXY, and in a special displayed box it stated:

– DOESN'T smoke or drink
– HATES to see girls cry
– SELDOM loses his temper
– WANTS to meet Elvis Presley
– ISN'T VIOLENT

The *Mirror* was obsessed with his eyes, calling them 'dark, luminous and slumberous', and writer Donald Zec commented how he found Cliff open-faced, well mannered and frank. The growing star's ambition was to buy his Mum and Dad a new house, star in films, and sell a million of one of his singles. As for Cliff's desire to meet Elvis, who was now in Germany, Zec commented: 'I would dearly love to be there at the time when wiggle meets wiggle on the banks of the Rhine.'

As for other happenings in 1959, The Drifters were called The Four Jets in America for the release in July of their own single, 'Jet Black', on which Cliff did not feature. So as not to be confused with the US Drifters. Scandinavia became the first overseas booking for Cliff in October, and Jet Harris married Carol Ann at St Paul's Church, Hounslow, in West London.

On disc Cliff had become less an outright rock 'n' roller and more a purveyor of love songs. 'Living Doll' from the film *Serious Charge* was the song which saw his appeal widen to encompass Mums and Dads as well as teenagers. From now on he was no rebel. He was a family entertainer.

Opposite: Checking through some antiques in London's Shepherd's Bush Market

Below: Years ago pop stars learnt to dance

Following pages: When you're riding high even shaving doesn't seem a chore

1959

1960

Opposite: At the Palladium in 1960, giving everything he's got. Hank is on the left

'I didn't know so much could happen in five months,' Cliff said in 1960 as he surveyed the period from January to May.

Uppermost in his mind was his first visit to the United States, but there were also rich memories of TV specials, awards, royal appearances and a season at the famous Palladium in London. His second film *Expresso Bongo* had opened in the States in March. There were records – hits of course. And there was the almighty row he had had with manager Tito Burns. It taught Cliff quite a lesson.

January 1960 had begun with an EP, his fourth. It was *Expresso Bongo* and featured 'Love', 'The Shrine on the Second Floor', 'A Voice in the Wilderness', and from The Shadows there was 'Bongo Blues'.

'A Voice in the Wilderness' also appeared as a single, along with 'Don't Be Mad at Me'. It was a song that Cliff disliked. 'I was never crazy about that number. Usually I know what I like by the simple way of saying to myself when I hear a new tune, "I'd buy that myself", Well, I didn't exactly dig Voice that much.'

His lack of feeling for the number gave rise to a major row with manager Tito Burns. Cliff was due to record the number in January for the very influential BBC TV show *Top of the Pops*. Tito did not go with him for the recording and Cliff decided he would sing the flip side. Later, when Tito learnt what Cliff had recorded, the music veteran went berserk. He knew Cliff had thrown away a great promotional moment and it was now unlikely that the record would make the top spot. Cliff said later: 'It might have done if I'd been a bit wiser at the time.'

America knocked Cliff out. He went there for the first time in January, a mere twenty-fours after achieving another milestone when with The Shadows he topped the bill on the *Sunday Night at the London Palladium* ATV show and had the legendary Platters on the same billing. He also heard he had been given the Carl-Alan award for recording the best-liked record of 1959, 'Living Doll'. And there was news that he would star in a London Palladium summer revue with other music luminaries of the time.

While he was in the US he heard that *NME* readers had voted him Britain's top male artiste and he flew back to London for an appearance at the then famous *NME* Poll-winners' Concert, which that year was held on 21 February. And just to put some cream on the cake – before he jetted back across the Atlantic – the same evening he again topped the bill on the very prestigious *Sunday Night at the London Palladium*.

He was in the US for five weeks and it was non-stop action from start to finish. He learnt quickly about the vastness of America, for while a few gigs meant a journey from one to the other of less than 100 miles, there were many where the distances almost reached five figures.

Cliff and the other artistes on the tour, who included Frankie Avalon, Bobby Rydell, Clyde McPhatter, Johnny and the Hurricanes, journeyed the US motorways (apparently they were an eye-opener to Cliff) in two lovely silver streamlined coaches, both with 'The biggest show of 1960' emblazoned on their sides. Most of the travel took place at night with the artistes either

sleeping on the coach or bedding down at a hotel during the morning and early afternoon preceding the sound check and evening concert performance.

'I thought I'd go all the way in America,' Cliff said at the time. 'At the end of the "Whole Lotta Shakin'" number I go down on one knee. But first I pull out a white handkerchief and lay it on the floor. The stages are so dirty that my trouser leg would be black if I didn't!' (He wore an all-white suit in the US instead of his usual black pants.)

For someone older it might have been an exhausting affair but nineteen-year-old Cliff found it exhilarating. Cliff's spot came during the show's second half. His Dad had travelled to the States and he and Tito observed closely the American acts. They advised the young Cliff to dispense with chat, plug the 'English' side strongly and work hard at the music. It seemed the right way.

While in America Cliff saw his US record company ABC-Paramount, talked to endless DJs and interviewers, and appeared on the *Pat Boone Show*. With Pat he sang a duet, 'Pretty Blue Eyes', and in Britain listeners to BBC's *Saturday Club* heard it on 5 March. Later, of course, he became a great friend of Pat Boone, with each in their way telling of their Christian faith.

Cliff's second film *Expresso Bongo* opened in New York on 15 March and there were, as in Britain, some good notices for Cliff. At the very least it was felt he had held his own.

March for Cliff in Britain meant his own television extravaganza on ATV, *Saturday Spectacular*, and he took part in BBC radio's *Royal Albert Hall Show*. On the 28th he was presented to Prince Philip, the Duchess of Kent and Princess Alexandra at the Odeon cinema in London's Leicester Square, the venue of the Royal Film Performance.

May saw Cliff in the Royal Variety Performance when he received another handshake from the Duke of Edinburgh, at the Victoria Palace, London, and also from the Queen. He also performed in a sketch, along with the Vernon Girls, entitled *Focus on Youth*. Two other pop stars of the moment, Lonnie Donegan and Adam Faith, appeared as well.

By June his ninth single, 'Please Don't Tease', had been released.

June to December saw the extraordinarily long season which Cliff and The Shadows spent in the London Palladium show *Stars in Your Eyes*. Cliff said: 'I don't mind admitting it is a long season but on the other hand we needed a prestige booking like this. It is a great honour.' He said he was not thrilled by writers describing him now as an all-round entertainer. Nor was he particularly pleased by stories of him earning vast sums of money and the inevitable speculation about whether he was worth, say, £50,000 a year, somewhat more than the sum earned by the Prime Minister. Cliff commented: 'I didn't put the price on my head, other people did. They must think I'm worth it, mustn't they! Because I sing rock 'n' roll and the girls all scream at me, some people think I'm a heathen or something.'

The Palladium event also starred Edmund Hockeridge, Russ Conway and Joan Regan.

While Cliff and The Shadows starred at the famous venue, the singles and albums continued to be released. And by now The Shadows had become recording artists in their own right with their classic single 'Apache', released in July, giving them top chart spots in many countries.

Away from immediate show-biz Cliff launched into a favourite hobby of his – buying cars. In August the press told of his realization of an ambition to own a £4,000 Ford car, the money for which had come from a £25,000 record royalty cheque he had received early in the month. It was also said that a magazine had paid £10,000 for his life story. Journalist Ron Evans commented that Cliff had already paid up his income tax for the next two years! Cliff kept a humble and somewhat downtrodden way of looking at things. He said he restricted himself to a spending wage of £10 per week. It seemed he even had some loose change by the week's end!

His £4,000 car was a Ford Thunderbird, a car favoured by other stars of the time, including Diana Dors and Eammon Andrews. The car had been resprayed in Cliff's favourite colour at the time, red. Evans reported that Cliff's company, Cliff Richard Entertainment Ltd, had grossed £10,000 in the last three months.

Fan mania continued during 1960 and newspapers dug hard for a Cliff story. One Sunday, *The People*, in its famous no-nonsense manner, brought fans and ex-managers together in a fine expansive piece of journalistic eye-catching screed: 'To the girls he's a heart-throb. To his two ex-managers CLIFF IS A HEART-BREAKER!'

Ex-manager John Foster was quoted as saying, 'Next time I'll get 'em under contract,' while Franklyn Boyd said of his dismissal, 'I've never been so stunned.'

The People's writer Peter Bishop believed the best person to reveal Cliff's backroom affairs was his Dad. He located him in the Palladium dressing-room. Mr Webb sipped a glass of beer, shook his head and told Bishop he was green in the music game and he just wanted the best advice he could find for his son. 'Foster? He didn't know enough about show business. Boyd? He didn't quite suit. He seemed to work my boy a bit hard. But Mr Burns now, we get along fine. He seems just right for my boy. But managers – you got to keep your eye on 'em.' Tito Burns was to be the next to go but not quite yet.

The girls' magazine *Valentine* was uninterested in whether one manager was better than another. In one of their pop specials which featured Cliff they said he had won his private war against success and it had made him one of the happiest young men in the recording business, 'Because the folk at the top were convinced if he left his favourite rock 'n' roll territory he would be snuffed out of the limelight as quick as lightning.' The 'folk at the top' were clearly wrong.

Valentine thought Cliff had snatched the teenage market right out of Tommy Steele's grip. Cliff's eyes – 'smouldering' – drew girls, they said,

like the bees and honey bit. They were warm and loving.

The feature was interesting and ranged from how the five foot ten inch Cliff was a little scared he might be on the plump side to his views on fans and on girls: 'He doesn't know the sort of girl she's going to be but he's got firm ideas about the sort of girl she's NOT going to be . . . ' The magazine commented on the 3,000 birthday cards he received when nineteen, and on his Mum and Dad and the house he had bought them.

His own room was described as a 'smart young room for one of today's top young men'. The stairs to his pad had floor-to-ceiling tubular banisters. The door was mushroom-shaped and the handle was shaped like a gramophone disc. Three walls were papered a sunshine yellow. The remaining wall had wallpaper crazily patterned with African scenes. There was a wardrobe and a side cupboard and the door and window frames were black.

This was the year Cliff left his teens and became twenty, but it was still pimples and not prospects that worried Cliff! He appeared on the ITV programme *Sunday Break* and was interviewed about his views on religion. He said it was a subject he and The Shadows often discussed. He said he had a great number of things to feel thankful for. The *NME Annual* for the year had Cliff's Mum telling how Dad had once upon a time said

that Cliff could not own a dog but Cliff had seen this little one in a Glasgow pet shop. He bought it and had it snuggled beneath his coat when he arrived home. Mum said Dad opened the door and succumbed to a smiling Cliff who said 'Do you mind?'

The year 1960 was on the whole a happy year, marred only slightly by the road accident which had injured Jet Harris and Hank Marvin in January. More saddening was the accident which killed Jack Conway, right-hand man to Tito, who left a widow and two children. And during 1960 there were five singles, six EPs and an album – rather more than most artistes had achieved.

Opposite: Early manager Tito Burns in his office

Below: With skiffle king Lonnie Donegan

Page 20: Another shot of Cliff from *Serious Charge*

Page 21: Taken at EMI record company offices

1961

He said his twentieth birthday was fantastic. He had never seen so many cards, telegrams and gifts. Ties, handkerchiefs and sweaters flooded his way. He could open a clothing shop. He was particularly impressed when the postman delivered an enormous box of exotic-looking cakes. They came from the South Sea Islands!

His twenty-first was doubly fantastic, not the least because so many people went out of their way to congratulate him. Pop papers issued special supplements or re-ordered their normal page structure to take his birthday into account, for in 1961 twenty-one marked the entry into real adult life, as opposed to the current eighteen.

Appropriately, EMI issued the album *21 Today*, but Cliff was holding and attending few parties. Business came first. Within hours of being twenty-one he was heading towards Australia for a major tour. He was realistic about the social scene. 'It wouldn't be possible to invite all the fans – I'd have to hire the Albert Hall to do that, and that wouldn't be very cosy.'

And there seemed to be no girl in his life with whom he could celebrate. Still, Cliff did say: 'I know howta kiss a girl but I'm just outa practice.'

Some of the musical journals reflected on his career. *NME*'s Derek Johnson, in a coming-of-age celebration supplement, said twenty-one was the age when most say goodbye to youth and step into manhood, but Johnson pointed out that Cliff had achieved more in his youth than most will pack into a lifetime. He thought it ironic that Cliff could now vote at an election and yet for three years had been an acknowledged show-biz great. He also reflected on Cliff's growing world influence and thought Cliff's message of goodwill had done much to cement friendship between different peoples of the world.

Johnson listed Cliff's achievements. There was his sky-rocketing rise into fame as the best-selling British artiste, the fact that every one of his fourteen singles (by 14 October, Cliff's birthday) had made the charts, and that 'Living Doll' had sold a million. There were amazingly successful tours in the Far East, Australia, South Africa and the United States. He had topped the bill of almost every major theatre and venue, and offers for his services poured in continually. He had appeared in the films *Serious Charge* and *Expresso Bongo* (*The Young Ones* was not yet on release), had been a show-stopper at three *NME* Wembley concerts, had successfully starred in numerous TV and radio shows, had appeared in a Royal Variety Performance and had graduated from a mere teenage idol into someone who had acquired a sophistication, polish and maturity which would normally be associated with a much older person.

Cliff's twenty-first birthday year witnessed more and more record hits and awards, and his first big film, *The Young Ones*. There was a change in The Shadows line-up and he acquired a new manager in Peter Gormley. This genial but thoroughly knowledgeable Australian is still with him. A very sad event was the death of Cliff's Dad.

The year 1961 opened as usual with new Cliff record material. His twelfth single 'Theme for a Dream', coupled with 'Mumblin' Mosie', led the way and was quickly followed by an EP, *Me and My Shadows*. In March it was officially announced that Peter Gormley would be Cliff's manager. It was the beginning of an era in which Cliff had clear and positive direction and which saw considerable trust grow between artiste and manager, a trust which would survive the usual ravages of the pop world.

In March Cliff and The Shadows were overseas, in South Africa, and then in the Far East, Australia and New Zealand. A map of their journeys in the early 1960s shows the enormous world coverage they achieved. They were welcomed everywhere and, before the advent of the Beatles, were the major British musical export.

On 15 May Cliff's father died of heart trouble, aged fifty-six. It seems that Cliff and his Dad were never close, yet Cliff admired his father. In Cliff's book, *It's Great to Be Young*, he

remarked how his success had made Dad and Mum a bit like a pair of teenagers. His father lived for the music and was gradually persuaded away from his job at Ferguson's to handle a million and one details of Cliff's show-biz career. He was part of the 'team' and as Cliff said: 'Of course it was difficult for a man to be employed by his son but that isn't the point. He's busier today than he's ever been. Nobody is quite what a Dad is to a boy, and even with Norrie and Tito, there were some things that I just couldn't go to them with.' But Dad died from a weak heart.

Drummer Tony Meehan's departure from The Shadows in October heralded the arrival of Brian Bennett. Meehan said he left because things had become 'too trite, too mechanical'. He had first met The Shadows in a Soho coffee shop. Born on 2 March 1942 in Hampstead, London, Meehan began his musical career with a £40 drum kit earning

And they're all his!

Below: With some fans, two and four-legged, in Australia

Opposite: A hectic dance sequence from *The Young Ones*

30s (£1.50) at the weekends and going to school on the weekdays. He became one of The Worried Men, Adam Faith's former group; he also spent time in Vince Taylor's Playboys and as one of The Vipers, a moderately successful skiffle group. Meehan tried other music partnerships after leaving The Shadows but in October the press reported that he had been signed by Sir Edward Lewis at Decca as an A&R man. His most famous partnership a few years later was with Jet Harris who, of course, had been a Shadow.

Change was inevitable in the Cliff camp, for things happened very fast there and in any case The Shadows were simultaneously developing their own career.

Summer saw a six-week season at Blackpool's Opera House, Meehan's last major appearances with The Shadows. During October and November Cliff and The Shadows

went 'down under' again as they consolidated their enormous popularity in Australia. In November there was a prestige booking at the Paris Olympia and in December came another major award for Cliff when he won the Variety Club of Great Britain's Show Business Personality of the Year Award.

Producer Norrie Paramor commented how he used to think he would never put rock on record for he wasn't sure England had the talent capable of doing it well. Cliff had changed his mind. He remarked how informality ruled at a Cliff recording and sometimes as many as twenty fans were allowed into the studio, for Cliff felt a small audience aided the creation of the necessary atmosphere. A session normally lasted three hours and on occasions fifty takes might be necessary but usually, Paramor said, things went smoothly.

Cliff was pragmatic about his work. He said he always found the question of what he might be doing five, ten or more years hence a bewildering one. It was simply a case of his being totally involved with what he was doing at the time. He admitted that he had moments of depression when he wondered about the future and that he couldn't contemplate his show-biz career collapsing! The only thing he thought he might find possible would be music publishing. As for marriage and family, his thoughts in 1961 were hardly domestic. 'Between the ages of twenty-five and twenty-seven would be the best time, in my view. By then I'd no longer be a kid, and would be ready to take on extra responsibilities.' His twenty-first birthday made him think he was a 'veteran', and in terms of the comings and goings in the music business it was a realistic assessment. His thoughts in this direction had been sparked off by someone remarking to him: 'Of course, you're an old-timer in show business now.'

He mused on how fame curtailed basic freedoms. 'It means I cannot say to myself, next Monday I'll do this, and that on Friday, because there are a great number of things to be considered before personal pleasure.'

He set out clearly his ideal year. He would like two major one-nighter tours of Britain, probably three weeks

in length each. He would spend a month in variety, set aside a number of weeks for planning and recording albums and singles, have anything up to two months playing by the seaside or a major provincial centre, and spend six more overseas, preferably including somewhere as yet unvisited. And each year he would make a film.

This year he starred in *The Young Ones*, which in its title song and overall presentation portrayed what some would term 'wholesome' youth without too many troubles and plenty of time for gaiety, fun and good clean loving. He had mixed feelings over the filming of *The Young Ones*. It gave him many happy memories and it was the first film he felt at ease making. However, he didn't cope at all well with the endless 'sitting at the side of the film set and waiting for my call to come on'.

It was his biggest role to date – of that he couldn't complain! He learnt an enormous amount from actor Robert Morley and he acquired the rudiments of dance. 'There were various routines in the movie – a soft shoe dance, chorus line and so on. I couldn't have coped with them when I first started on the production.' But the boredom of inactivity! It seemed such a waste of time to someone bursting with energy and vitality.

His first reading of the script worried him, mainly because of the dance requirement, but the cast was young and that encouraged him.

Cliff played Nicky, a very trendy individual who adored tight jeans and loud searing music. Nicky led a youth club in London's Paddington area. The club met in a rather run-down hut but it was pleasant enough for Nicky, girlfriend Toni (played by Carole Gray), and members. None of the members knew that Nicky's father was a rich millionaire property owner by the name of Hamilton Black, played in the film by Robert Morley.

The secret came out when – unknown to Nicky – Dad decided he would redevelop the area where the youth club had their hut, which would naturally mean demolition of the premises. They could keep the land only if they paid £1,500, five years' rent in advance. To help raise the money the youth club staged a concert at which Nicky revealed his vocal prowess. Dad was so impressed he promised to build them a new club.

The Young Ones met enormous box-office success and made all the months of work worthwhile. The album and singles from it sold heavily and quickly. Cliff remarks: 'I think it was a peak in my life because I'd never sold records so fast.' The single (the film's title song) had advance orders of over 300,000. Within days of its release sales had zoomed towards the million mark and the song was topping the charts. The film was the event of 1961 for Cliff fans.

1961

1962

The film *Summer Holiday* was the main attraction of 1962 in the Cliff Richard story. Otherwise there were the expected hit records, awards, meetings with royalty, radio and television bookings, and personnel changes.

The most explosive story was that of Cliff's impending marriage to a seventeen-year-old, Valerie Stratford. She told the press she was going to marry him. Cliff said the idea was crazy. Valerie's church in Willesden echoed to the reading of the banns and a wedding present list was circulated. Cars were arranged and all was set for 10 February. Fleet Street nationals assembled their scribes in hungry anticipation, tempered with the usual but necessary cynicism about the whole affair.

Saturday the 10th was a non-event. Cliff didn't make it to the church on time or at any time. Valerie, owner of 3,500 pictures of Cliff, had to admit it was all a hoax.

Not unexpectedly, magazines and journals devoted the early part of the year to questioning Cliff about the kind of girl he might really want. Cliff spoke out.

He wanted the kind of girl who his mother had said all along would be the right sort. Grooming and good manners were two essential qualities from the girl of his choice, as well as cooking and housekeeping skills. He disliked too much make-up, particularly theatrical eye shadow, too revealing fashions, over-bleached hair, ridiculous hairstyles, and mile-long fingernails. Cliff said boys didn't mind looking at girls like this but they wouldn't dream of marrying one. He had little time for girls who looked and acted too loud, smoked too much, drank too much and used bad language. He put it tersely: 'Too often a girl is smart intellectually, and yet stupid socially.' It was hard stuff.

He wanted a girl who was a good mixer socially, was willing to share his interests and knew how to give and take. Petting was not approved of. A career girl was out, for the 'girl I marry must want a normal family life with children . . . I want the kind of girl I would be proud to bring home to meet my mother and sister – a girl who will be as proud of me as I am of her.'

At the beginning of the year Cliff

Right: Into the mood and feel of the song

Far right: A lovely, expressive shot of Cliff and comedian Sid James

Page 28: He sings off stage as well!

Page 29: At the Shepherd's Bush Theatre dressing-room: a case of grab a bite and back to the action

reflected in the magazine *Hit Parade* on his movements during the previous twelve months. *The Young Ones* dominated his conversation; so also did his travels, particularly in Australia and South Africa. Much to his surprise his arrival in Australia was greeted with heavy rain! Eventually the skies cleared and the fans rapidly responded to Cliff and The Shadows. The result of the trip was a doubling of sales in Australia.

South Africa had seen the premiere of *The Young Ones* on 24 December, which Cliff attended. He was met by superb weather and great hospitality.

The main departure from the Cliff Richard scene in 1962 was guitarist Jet Harris. He made his last appearance backing Cliff with The Shadows on 15 April when Cliff yet again appeared at the *New Musical Express* Poll-winners' Concert at Wembley. Liquorice Locking replaced Jet. He was to have a considerable impact over the next few years on Cliff's religious beliefs.

On 22 April, when Liquorice made his debut in Blackpool with The Shadows, Bruce Welch collapsed. He had a septic throat. Pete Carter became his temporary replacement during the ensuing variety week in Liverpool.

This year saw The Shadows become the first group from Britain to win a gold disc for sales of over a million of their classic instrumental 'Apache'. Cliff and The Shadows also met Princess Margaret and Lord Snowdon during an evening at Eton College Mission's Youth Club in Hackney.

Sunday Night at the London Palladium was one of the television events of the year. while in terms of live performances there was a summer season in July and August at the ABC, Blackpool.

Summer Holiday dominated the year, however. Filming to take place in May and June. It was shot in five countries and entailed 3,000 miles of travel.

'The girl I have in mind for the film must be the type of girl who will bring out the lover instinct in Cliff,' said Ken Harper, producer of *Summer Holiday* and of *The Young Ones*.

'After what Ken did for me in *The Young Ones*,' said Cliff, 'anything he decides is OK by me. For let's face it – this is only a film. Ken's looking for a co-star for me, not a bride.' Lauri Peters was chosen.

Cliff, along with his glamorous co-star, flew to Athens in a BEA Comet on 28 May. The film was a happy story about the adventures of a gang of boys and girls who journey across Europe on a London Transport bus! Cliff was one of the bus mechanics who had originally been given the task of overhauling the bus and driving it over to the Continent.

There were numerous photogenic film locations, including dusty stone-coloured Yugoslavian villages, historic Athens and the rich blue seas of the Aegean. There were fourteen song and dance numbers and Cliff sang vocals in eight. He made personal

1962

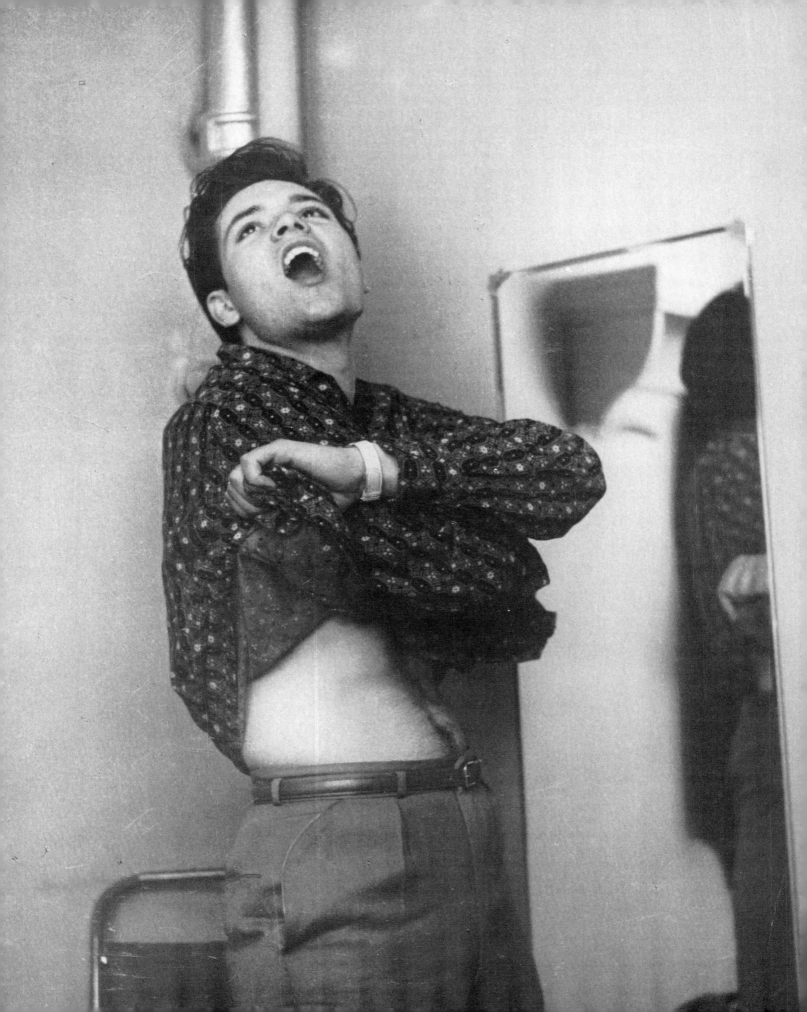

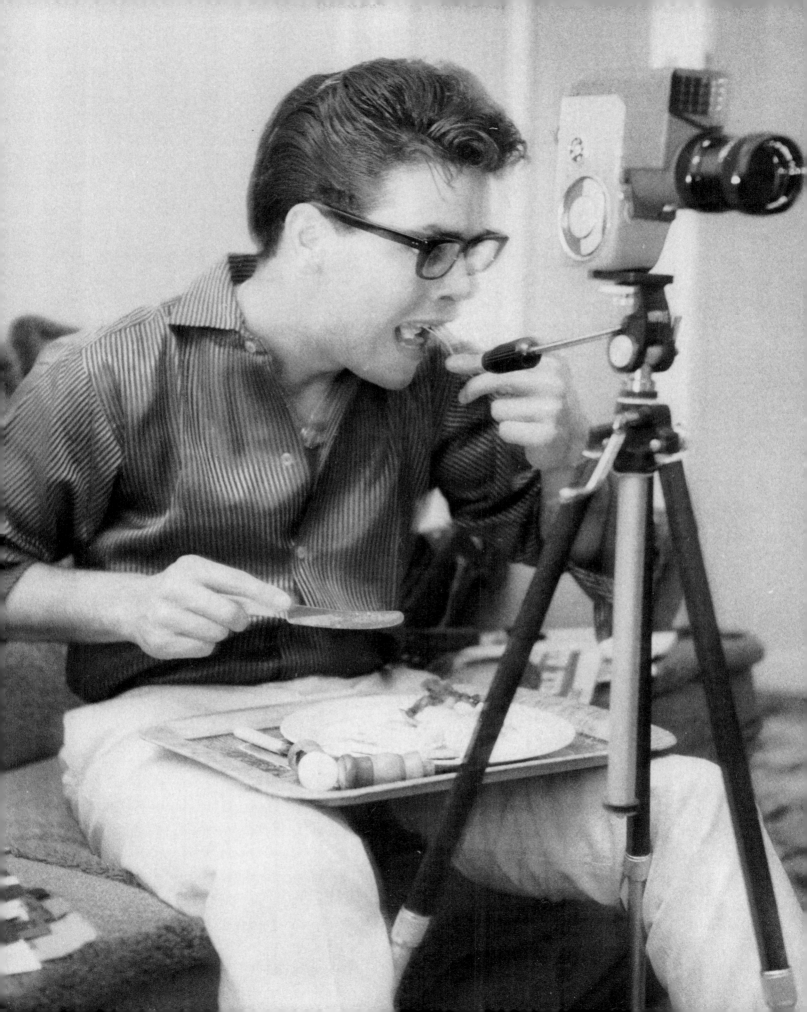

history by emerging as a songwriter, for he helped write two songs in the film. One was the enormously popular, and smash single hit, 'Bachelor Boy', penned with Bruce Welch, and the other, with Mike Conlin, was entitled 'Big News'. 'It's always been an ambition of mine to write,' Cliff said at the time.

An unusual star of the filming and film was Trudy, a huge dog who resembled some form of wild lion! Trudy, who became a male called Charlie in the film, attached herself to Cliff and followed him everywhere.

Cliff found filming exhausting. He was usually up by five-thirty in the morning and he was working in temperatures of a hundred or so most days. But life was made particularly pleasant by the fact that his family were holidaying in Greece and he saw rather more of them than he might have done even in England. He had rented a beach villa near Athens for his mother and two sisters.

In Chris Hutchins' short paperback, *Life With Cliff Richard*, published in 1963, Norrie Paramor recalled how each and every moment in Greece seemed to be filled with some kind of film action, but one Sunday the entire cast was given the day off. 'Cliff hired a boat, a magnificent one, and took everybody out to a wonderful island; it was the day in a lifetime for many of them and must have cost Cliff a small fortune.'

It was all done unobtrusively and no one knew, though Norrie found out a few days later, that Cliff had financed the trip. 'That's like Cliff; always so unassuming. He will often come round to my house and perhaps arrive as we are having dinner. But my wife Joan has to invite him to have some soup with us and then slip a plate of food in front of him or he would think that he was taking something he shouldn't.

'Above all he has humility – the humility to listen and take advice even though he has firmness of opinion. In his position he could easily throw his weight about and make demands – but he never does.'

Summer Holiday received its British premiere in January 1963. Cliff's two songs for the film certainly inspired him to greater writing activity. He told readers of *Hit Parade* that he found writing a great source of pleasure and satisfaction. 'I'm conscious of the fact that I shall never be a top-class composer. But I hope that I shall be able to continue

turning out a few more of my efforts from time to time.'

He recalled that he had written 'Happy Like a Bell' with Cherry Wainer and how Patti Brook had recorded one of his songs, 'I Love You, I Need You'. 'I know that I don't have the ability to produce a song like "The Young Ones". They don't come like this very often, and naturally I'm very delighted that it fell to me to exploit it – though I have to admit that I didn't rate its chances very highly when it was first suggested to me for single release!'

And Cliff graciously admitted, when it was pointed out to him, that he had thought the same about 'Living Doll' and look what had happened to that!

In another issue of *Hit Parade* Cliff talked about his likes and dislikes.

Elvis still ranked high in his list of favourite male singers, with Rick Nelson and Ray Charles also being named. Connie Francis, sultry sensuous Julie London, and Helen Shapiro made the 'girl' section. Apparently he still enjoyed reading in front of a blazing fire while a storm raged outside and trying to accompany records on his guitar. As for dislikes, he hated smoking, underground trains, and having to turn on the mechanical smile for photographers.

Indian curry and rice emerged, not surprisingly, under 'favourite foods', while Tizer and ice-cream won the drink category. Green was his favourite colour now and 'anything casual' for clothes. His weight was given as 11st 9lb, height 5ft 10½ in, hair black, eyes dark brown.

1962

Happy times on *Summer Holiday*

1963

Below: The film premiere he missed

Opposite: Sun and body talk at Sidges, near Barcelona

Page 34: Twentieth-century star meets famous name from the past

Page 35: Picture session in the woods near Bournemouth

The year 1963 could have been disastrous for Cliff. He had reigned at the top of British pop for four-and-a-half years. He deserved a rest, yet suddenly he found he had to work harder than ever. For 1963 saw the arrival of the Beatles. Their phenomenal success was accompanied by a mighty avalanche of singers and groups from Merseyside in particular and the North in general. Each of them posed a potential threat to Cliff as Britain's number one pop singer.

Hitherto Cliff and a small handful of others had withstood the domination of British charts and music halls by American acts. Now the situation was reversed. Suddenly 'good' meant British, and this applied in America as well as in Britain. For Cliff there was no time to relax if he was to retain the affection of, and sales to, thousands. So 1963 was another year of hard work, with hit singles, TV specials, awards, travel overseas – much the same as usual. But one trip overseas was very special. This was to Kenya where Cliff had for several years enjoyed remarkable popularity. This was in large part due to the British Forces Broadcasting Service

and in particular to a DJ called Keith Skues. BFBS was heard by the resident population and not merely British troops. Another different and important facet of the year lay in rumours of a romance for Cliff. Whereas the one of 1962 was fictitious this new revelation seemed very real.

Whatever the competition might be as 1963 progressed, Cliff's hard work of 1962 gave him an important boost early in the year.

On 10 January *Summer Holiday* was premiered in London at the Odeon, Leicester Square. Cliff and his entourage were due to arrive at the cinema in a London Transport bus, as in the film, but the square was so full that Cliff was advised to come by car. Cliff had carefully avoided seeing any run-throughs of the film for he thought it would be a good idea to see it for the first time at the premiere. Sadly and to his great disappointment even the idea of arriving in a black Cadillac was in the event out of the question because of the crowds. The star of the show ended up watching television in manager Peter Gormley's flat, but at least he made it to the private party given by promoter

Leslie Grade at the Orchid Room of London's Dorchester Hotel after the film. 'You didn't have to queue you know,' was fellow actor Melvin Hayes' cheerful greeting. 'They'd have let you into the cinema if you'd told them who you were!' The party went well and after dinner Cliff and Alma Cogan gave EMI head, Sir Joseph Lockwood, a lesson in the intricacies of the Locomotion dance.

The film was an enormous success and after its spell at the Odeon it moved a few doors away to the Rialto where it drew vast crowds. When the film went on general release the cinemas were packed. Reviews were favourable. One, by *Daily Mirror* man Peter Yates, suggested that Cliff had a natural flair and the right range of facial expressions for comedy. A bus driver at London Transport's Chiswick depot said of Cliff's driving: 'If he ever flops as a singer he can always become a bus driver.'

January was the month when *Summer Holiday*'s soundtrack came out in album form and The Shadows entered the charts at number one with 'Dance On'. There was also a 'new-look' Cliff on television. The event was the 6 January showing of *Sunday Night at the London Palladium*. Instead of relying on The Shadows for his sole backing Cliff worked with some dancers plus the Michael Sammes Singers. Each song was a mini-production number. During his short set Cliff sang 'Moonlight Bay' with singers and dancers. He was with The Shadows for 'Bachelor Boy', two of the group joined him on the spiritual 'Toll the Bell Easy', and then with a girl on either side he launched into 'Dancing Shoes'.

The *Mirror* of 7 January carried the extraordinary story of the sealed package which secretly left a West End barber's shop every fortnight. *Mirror* man Donald Zec said it contained the newly-clipped hair from Cliff's head. And we were reminded of how Cliff had been voted by *Motion Picture Herald* 'Britain's most popular film star of 1962'.

During 1963 Cliff became known as 'The Sunshine Boy' because of his visits to sunny places. South Africa was the first. He and The Shadows began their tour on 16 January. Kenya followed in February and some months later he won the Kenya Hit

1963

33

The plaque reads:

A
DOMENICO
THEOTOCOPVLI
EL GRECO
1548-1624

Parade Popularity Poll. Later in the year he visited New Zealand, Australia, Spain and Israel, where a cavalcade of 100 teenage motor-cyclists escorted Cliff from Tel Aviv's Lydda airport to his hotel. 'We had to drive at a dangerous speed to shake them off,' said Cliff, and there were scores of fans who, commando-like, climbed down ropes which hung from the airport balcony.

His Kenya visit was punctuated by a special charity concert at Mitchell Park given on 11 February at the request of African leader Tom Mboya. Cliff arrived in Kenya in the early hours of the morning and stayed at the famous Norfolk Hotel. 'It was a marvellous event,' said Cliff, a few months later. 'The hospitality was first class and I would like to make a return visit.'

His visit to Kenya followed an exhausting four-week tour of South Africa – 'Just fabulous' said a suntanned Cliff. 'Sometimes there were as many as 12,000 with banners and screaming – you know. It was fantastic. Really fabulous.'

He returned from South Africa and Kenya on Valentine's Day and there to greet him at London Airport was the love of his life – Mum!

He was questioned about apartheid by reporters and his response was that he hadn't really been aware of the problem. He spoke of two concerts where he played before Indian and African people and said the reception was great. He felt things would sort themselves out in South Africa.

Nine days later Cliff began a tour of forty-two one-night stands in Britain, travelling by special coach on the inevitable long and tiring journeys. The aim was simple – to keep in contact with fans, for this was Beatle year. It was estimated that around 200,000 people would hear him and he might sign as many as 4,000 autographs. There would be the usual interviews with the media and occasionally one out of the ordinary. An example of this occurred in the West Country when Cliff was interviewed for a youth club magazine by Minehead clergyman the Reverend Bryan Bennett who questioned Cliff about his lifestyle, beliefs and show business in general.

The June–September holiday season at Blackpool entailed a great deal of rehearsing because Cliff and The Shadows were appearing in the new £350,000 ABC Theatre's show which took the form of a travelogue of the world's entertainment centres and The Shadows and Cliff kept popping up in the story. Some £40,000 was spent on advertising Cliff and The Shadows. They were most impressed with the dressing rooms. 'Let's live here,' said Hank Marvin. 'Who wants to do the show?' The sun refused to shine during the sixteen weeks they were in Blackpool and Cliff failed to have even one swim. While the rain poured down he recorded the album *When In France!* While in Blackpool he and Bruce wrote 'Don't Talk to Him'.

In August Jet Harris, who had teamed up with Tony Meehan, produced the top five hit single 'Applejack' for Decca, but early in September Harris, along with vivacious and talented Billie Davis, was injured in a car crash when their vehicle was in collision with a bus near Evesham, Worcestershire. The same month Bruce Welch said he was leaving The Shadows on doctor's advice. Cliff commented: 'I am shattered. I suppose the inevitable has happened. We all knew Bruce drove himself too hard.'

For Cliff there was supposed love for the startlingly good-looking Jackie Irving, twenty years old, a brunette and one of the Pamela Davis Dancers. Cliff told the press how he enjoyed her company enormously, 'which is why most of my dates are with her'. He had known Jackie for some time. But – sadly, some close associates would say – nothing came of it and later Jackie married pop star Adam Faith.

Cliff's new house had been purchased a year back but the family only moved in during the November of 1963. It cost £30,000 and was a six-bedroomed Tudor-style mansion with eleven acres of land, situated in Upper Nazeing, Essex. Hi-fis littered the place, chrome was much in evidence, and Mum had a see-through oven door, a rotisserie and a plate warmer. Cliff had a snooker room. One neighbour, asked for her views on having a pop star living in the peaceful hamlet of Upper Nazeing, said: 'Provided he's not a communist or anything like that I think it's marvellous.'

Cliff's Mum spoke to the magazines and summed up her views on parenthood with the one word 'honesty', while Cliff told *Record Pictorial* that it didn't matter whom he married provided she was the right kind of girl, which did not say a great deal but then Cliff must have been heartily weary of the question by now. He also told of the responsibility which he felt towards his family and of how it was his duty to do his best by his mother. He said he had for some time wanted a residence where things could be relatively peaceful: 'Naturally I'd be happiest if the fans would appreciate me wanting a bit of private life.'

The press, according to Cliff, got a few things wrong about the residence. One major dispute concerned reports that there were guards everywhere with Alsatians straining at the leash. Cliff said the stories originated with his chauffeur who had a sense of humour. He was taken seriously although he had made up the stories. Cliff's only sadness about his new house revolved around whether he would see much of it in view of his heavy schedule. 'I suppose I'll only be home a few times a year.'

In the Radio Luxembourg *Book of Stars* Cliff told young fans they should work at being themselves and be different. He stressed the importance of having a genuine interest in people, an ability to see someone else's viewpoint, an inner warmth, a pleasant disposition and a natural smile.

After a holiday and medical treatment Bruce Welch returned to The Shadows in October, but Liquorice Locking made his final appearance with The Shadows on *Sunday Night at the London Palladium* on 3 November. Liquorice felt religious work was his calling. Cliff found this attitude impressive, and he had been deeply affected by the Jehovah's Witness faith of the guitarist. Some of Cliff's family became Jehovah's Witnesses but later Cliff came to think that the movement was in error.

Cliff survived 1963. He had played the States in August and he had appeared on the all-important US *Ed Sullivan Show*. And there was also one other important step taken in 1963 – filming began on *Wonderful Life*, on which Liquorice helped with the recording. The filming continued into 1964, but that's another year . . .

Opposite: Recording in Portugal: Peter Gormley is seated left, Hank rubs his chin, Norrie confers

Below: On the famed Ed Sullivan US TV show in 1963

1963

1964

Cliff and the Beatles, Cliff and Jackie Irving, Cliff and a new girl called Lonanne Richards, and Cliff playing King Canute were just some of the subjects which caught the attention of Fleet Street in 1964.

More important was the film *Wonderful Life*, which began the year, and Cliff's star role in the pantomime *Aladdin and His Wonderful Lamp*, which ended it.

Cliff had heard the news that he would be filming *Wonderful Life* in 1963 – on his birthday. It was also the day he had met co-star Susan Hampshire for the first time. They were introduced in his manager's office in Savile Row in London, where there was a press conference and much bustle, so much so that the champagne remained unopened on the desk. Susan had given Cliff a present – a bottle-opener, appropriately enough!

Wonderful Life swung into operation during December 1963 and the filming carried on into January.

'We've put a lot of hard work into our new film,' said Cliff. 'In fact I'd go as far as to say that this is the most adventurous movie we've made. There are all kinds of great scenes in it, like a take-off of the James Bond thriller *Dr No* and impressions of a lot of Hollywood epics seen in the past few years.'

He acquired a tan while filming and a chance to stretch out, and the golden sand of the Canaries was something he well remembered.

The film itself was seen as an amusing and escapist story accompanied by breezy, bouncing and romantic song-and-dance numbers set against the gorgeous scenery of north-west Africa. Apart from Cliff and leading lady Susan Hampshire, the film had Walter Slezak, Dennis Price and The Shadows. And there were the by-now regular bunch – of Melvyn Hayes, Richard O'Sullivan and Una Stubbs. One major newcomer was former Miss Israel, Alizia Gur.

The story is about a group of youngsters who find themselves temporarily stranded in the Canary Islands. They become involved with an old-time film director who is shooting a spectacular epic. Their youth and vitality contribute towards him producing a hit film.

The film received its premiere at the Empire, Leicester Square in London on 2 July. Princess Alexandria and Angus Ogilvy attended, and so, this time, did Cliff! Proceeds went to the National Association of Youth Clubs.

A major book on the film was written by Dick Tathan, and there was a soundtrack album and singles. Needless to say all the constituents made for one big success.

It was the premiere which set the newspaper scribes wondering whether Cliff had a new girl in his life. When he arrived at the cinema it was with dark-haired eighteen-year-old Lonanne, a dancer. Cliff was dressed in a navy blue evening suit and a light blue frilled shirt. He denied there was any romance, and the attractive eighteen-year-old smiled when Cliff said she was a very good dancer, had appeared in the film, and was a good friend. She added, 'But, I don't dance with Cliff.'

Cliff's favourite story from his filming experiences centres around an English nurse they met in the Canary Islands. She had come there some three years previously and had only a hazy idea of what was happening in Britain. Since she was English and also spoke Spanish she had been offered and had accepted the job of nurse with the *Wonderful Life* unit. She beseiged The Shadows with enquiries about the Beatles and their hit songs. The result was that The Shadows, about to film *Wonderful Life*, had to give her a twenty-minute concert of Beatle songs!

The pantomime *Aladdin* was fun and it furthered Cliff's growing reputation as a family entertainer. The Shadows, Cliff, Arthur Askey and Una Stubbs provided the artiste base. The Shadows provided the musical score. It was the group's second pantomime and their second season at the Palladium. It was a great box office triumph.

'I wasn't at all bored during the entire run. We had a lot of fun, we were in good spirits and I just enjoyed doing it,' said Cliff. He was also concerned with his future appeal. 'I want to keep the teenage fans and also work on older fans. We're not has-beens at twenty-three. I hope things are just starting. I want always to make records.'

Fans, though, can be irksome, and during 1964 there were one or two moments when they were.

Opposite: Lucky Cliff with co-star Susan Hampshire in *Wonderful Life*

1964

'I'm grateful to my fans,' Cliff said, but added, 'there's always an element who don't know where to draw the line. I came home once to find a group of girls having tea in the kitchen.'

And there was the astonishing and rather sad affair at his sister's wedding. Pat McDonland, who had worked for Tito Burns and become Cliff's secretary, told a woman's magazine in 1964 how fans had caused Cliff great pain. Thousands had besieged the church where Donna was being married, her veil had been torn off and her exquisite dress all crumpled. Cliff had said to Pat McDonland: 'They don't understand, Pat. This is Donna's day. She's the star of the show, not me.'

This was, thankfully, an isolated event.

In 1964 Cliff met wild acclaim and a response which rivalled the Beatles' reception during his dates in May in Denmark and especially Copenhagen. Extra concerts were hurriedly arranged. Cliff and The Shadows had not changed, but the music world around them had. Yet they were still

meeting unbridled enthusiasm and even topped the charts at the end of the year with 'The Minute You're Gone', a song Cliff had recorded in Nashville during the summer of 1963.

As for those other interests mentioned by Fleet Street, in February Jackie Irving said: 'I don't see Cliff any more.' She said that while Cliff was away filming she had not received 'a letter, a postcard, nothing.' She denied there had ever been any romance. They were friends, nothing more. 'I have plenty of other boyfriends and I realize it wouldn't do Cliff's career any good at all if he got married. It would only annoy his fans.'

On the Beatles, Cliff said: 'All they've done is to revert to rock 'n' roll. Actually, it's fab all right, but it's really five-year-old music. Course they're very wild and raucous. We've played the whole thing down, the screaming and the raving. The Beatles have stoked the whole thing up again.'

Cliff called Beatle material 'home-made' music and also said: 'Anybody

who can shout can be a Beatle.' It was good journalistic copy, as was Cliff's comment: 'Of course the Beatles are our biggest competitors, but I've told the boys not to care. I think we make a better sound and we've got far more polish than the Beatles.' Cliff fans grunted in approval.

There was also the matter of Cliff's love scene with a dripping Susan Hampshire in *Wonderful Life* which surprised some people, but after all he had done something similar with Lauri Peters in *Summer Holiday*, though Cliff said at the time: 'I'm always a little uneasy during rehearsals when the technicians are looking on.'

In the real life love stakes of 1964 former Shadows man Jet Harris learnt from Billie Davis that their romance was at an end, and he was also divorced by wife Carol.

Cliff and The Shadows played across Europe, Britain, Scandinavia, and in the summer performed at Great Yarmouth for a change, rather than Blackpool.

The special events of 1964 included the Royal Variety Show, an ATV

one-hour special, an appearance on German TV in Munich and stories of Leslie Grade, Cliff's agent, turning down invitations for Cliff to appear at celebrated night spots including the Desert Inn, Las Vegas.

The ATV programme attracted the most interest. It was entitled *Cliff and The Shadows* and was initially kept off the screen by a strike. However, it was re-scheduled for 9.40 pm on Wednesday, 15 July, and replaced the advertised documentary *Fans, Fans, Fans!* – a programme on the history of mass adulation.

Cliff's special guest was Liza Minnelli, the talented daughter of legendary Judy Garland. She flew to London especially for the programme and it was her first British appearance.

The programme was a change from the more normal format offered by Cliff and The Shadows – the solid rostrum of the neatly posed group playing a sequence of three or four instrumental numbers and songs, with the host of the show saving a spot for the star guest's solo. This was replaced by a programme with a story-line through which ran a touch of musical comedy. There was a good opportunity to observe Cliff and The Shadows as individuals and not just as the star and his backing group. Cliff sang songs like 'Constantly' and 'True True Loving', there were excerpts from *Wonderful Life* and numbers from it included 'Swinging Affair' and the title theme. Liza sang 'Meantime' as a solo and joined with the Pamela Davis Dancers for a big production number.

Another 'special' was Cliff's appearance in The Shadows' film *Rhythm and Green*. He played King Canute.

Beatles or no Beatles, Stones or no Stones, Cliff and The Shadows marched on successfully through 1964. Perhaps those who liked the Beatles or dug the Stones appreciated little of Cliff's musical world, but there were still enough who did for whom Cliff was the tops.

1964

Opposite: A joyous Cliff with a satisfied Una Stubbs in *Aladdin*

Left: Sight-seeing in Europe, 1964

1965

Readers of the largest British music weekly for young people, the *New Musical Express*, may have been aware of John, Paul, George and Ringo but it didn't dissuade them from voting Cliff their World Top Male Singer in the poll of 1964. They even cast Elvis aside. It augured well for 1965.

NME writer Derek Johnson analysed Cliff in the 1965 *NME Annual*. He traced Cliff's story back to those first exciting heady days of 'Move It' in 1958 and said how people assumed he was part and parcel of a music scene where people came and went overnight and rested on their laurels after one hit record.

Johnson said a small band of artistes with genuine talent, 'star

Below: Another award, but they still smile as if it's the first. The late John Rostill is far left

Below right: Auditioning for Tarzan, in Portugal

quality', lasted. There was Tommy Steele and Adam Faith. Cliff, he thought, more than any other, had convincingly consolidated his position as an international star and, eventually, a mass-appeal family performer.

Cliff at that time was seen to possess world chart status greater than any recording artist anywhere – with the exception then of the Beatles. And Cliff had recorded in other languages and not relied on his English versions.

Johnson put it simply: 'The truth is, in Cliff's case – you name it, he's done it.' Johnson could see no reason why success and yet more success should not come Cliff's way.

There was one snag, at least if seen purely in show-business terms: Cliff was becoming increasingly involved with his search for self. During the autumn of 1965 his commitment as a practising Christian became absolute – so says his mentor of the time and the first chronicler of his life, David Winter. And this was nine months or so away from the moment when Cliff appeared on stage at a Billy Graham evangelist meeting and announced that he was a Christian. Then the whole world knew. At this point in 1965 friends were aware, show-business writers sniffed, and the man himself was becoming increasingly fulfilled. It meant he was spending time with religious groups rather than

in the studios or on tour. The world's top male pop singer, according to *NME* readers, actually became an assistant leader of his church's Crusaders group in December 1965. And he spent part of his holidays cruising the Broads with young people. Winter says the girls giggled at first and the boys were tongue-tied but soon everyone accepted Cliff as a friendly human being rather than an awesome world-famous singer with fans who would give their all to be in the youth fellowship of St Paul's Anglican Church in North London!

Yet 1965 was not without the usual array of successful pop world activities. Cliff and The Shadows

1965

recorded three one-hour specials for ATV. On the tenth anniversary edition of *Thank Your Lucky Stars* Cliff received a gold disc for 'Bachelor Boy'. In the United States he again recorded for the American top-rated show-business TV programme, the *Ed Sullivan Show*, and with The Shadows he appeared in yet another Royal Variety Show with orchestra and guitars as backing. They turned down an offer to appear at the Royal Command Performance for they did not wish to be part of a special 'Focus on Pop' section. Certainly both were too big an act for consideration as one 'filler' among others in a general look at the music scene.

The 1964 pantomime *Aladdin and His Wonderful Lamp* carried over into 1965 and ended at the Palladium on 10 March. Cliff then flew to Portugal for a brief holiday which he broke off for his Broads Christian week, after which he returned to Portugal.

He had a Continental tour with The Shadows which began at Frejus on 7 July and ended in Geneva, Switzerland, on 16 July. His summer show-business activities centred on Southend at the end of July and Bournemouth early in August. The latter month saw his catchy 'Lucky Lips' hit the top spot in six countries: Hong Kong, Sweden, Norway, Israel, Holland and South Africa.

Early in September he played a charity show at the ABC Northampton which donated proceeds to the rebuilding of Milton Keynes Church. October saw Cliff overseas once more with one date at the Roma Theatre in Warsaw, Poland, on the 11th.

Cliff's career had already lasted long enough to warrant 'career' programme specials and in October, the completion of Cliff's seventh successful year, the BBC Light Programme (the radio channel which broadcast some pop music before Radio One got off the ground) ran *The Cliff Richard Story*.

His Christmas performances for 1965 were confined to television and an appearance on the TV show *Once Upon a Wishbone*. He had decided to free himself from the lengthy commitment demanded in rehearsing and then presenting the pantomime extravaganza.

The least expected event of the year was his decision to go back to his school, Cheshunt Secondary Modern, to give a concert on 4 December in aid of school funds.

Cliff's increasing religious involvement was not surprising. He and The Shadows argued the pros and cons of belief far into the night while on tour. Former Shadow Liquorice Locking had given Cliff a taste of the Scriptural treasures waiting to be found, although Cliff, unlike Liquorice, his sisters and Mum, was not to become a Jehovah's Witness. At first Cliff seemed impressed by the change this religious movement had made in their lives but later he became increasingly critical of its beliefs and saddened by its adoption by those nearest and dearest to him. The difference of religious faith in such a close-knit family was obviously disturbing.

Cliff's articles, which appeared in various magazines and journals, had become more serious as time progressed. He was concerned about values and ideals, the behaviour of young people in society. His views seemed quite conservative. He was relatively unconcerned about political and social questions and he had no real argument for continuing to play in South Africa other than that he felt it right he should do so.

His financial holdings attracted considerable press interest. Constellation Investment took over the companies which he and Frank Ifield owned and the press reckoned the take-in was in the region of almost £500,000 per annum. It was deduced from this that Cliff must be a millionaire.

Financial 'pros' and 'cons' were of marginal interest to hard-core fans. Their main concern was whether Cliff's increasing religious activity would lead him to the point where he felt show business could no longer feature in his life. And The Shadows must have been wondering about their future. They could certainly go solo in view of their many record successes, but to leave Cliff would end one of Britain's most famous musical partnerships ever.

These conjectures and worries would come to a head the following year.

1965

It was in 1966 that Cliff's Mum, aged forty-five, married a young man of twenty-four.

In the same year fans cried and wrote pleading letters, for it seemed as though Cliff would give up show business and become a religious education teacher. He was reported making visits to a teacher training college and Cliff told the world: 'We haven't decided anything yet, but Dr Theakston has said that he would be delighted to have me as a trainee.' The alarm had begun the evening he appeared on stage with American evangelist Billy Graham and told the world that he was a Christian and that his Christian faith had affected the way he looked at life and living.

This was the year of the film *Finders Keepers*, of appearing in the guise of a puppet for a film called *Thunderbirds Are Go*, of discussing whether he would play concerts behind the Iron Curtain, of deciding he would after all commit himself to a lengthy pantomime season when he played in *Cinderella* at the London Palladium. During 1966 Cliff had his first taste of cabaret at a legendary night spot; he made four singles, four EPs and two albums, and appeared in special TV shows for both BBC and the independent network – it was a busy year even without Mum re-marrying and without the anguish of his fans!

Mrs Webb became Mrs Bodkin at a registry office on 18 June. Her husband Derek had been Cliff's chauffeur. Cliff didn't know. He was told after the ceremony. That evening the surprised Cliff held a press conference. The two could have his E-type Jaguar for their honeymoon. He said of Derek: 'I can hardly call him Dad!' He said he was not worried by the age difference. He said Derek was an old friend. But he was a trifle stunned by it all.

The reception was strictly a family affair and took place at Rockwood, Cliff's Upper Nazeing home. Cliff, his sisters and Derek's parents were virtually the only people present. Why was Mum so secretive? 'Mum told me that the reason she kept it all a secret was that she didn't want it to be a show-biz wedding with lots of people there. She wanted to be married quietly and this was the only way she could do it. She wanted just to be plain Mrs Webb getting married and not Cliff Richard's Mum.'

Naturally the press asked Cliff whether he had marriage plans. The answer was pretty short: 'No.'

The wedding meant that Cliff was left with too large a house, and he put it up for sale. Early in September the rumoured buying price was almost £44,000. He bought his new parents a house at Highfield Drive, Broxbourne, Hertfordshire, as a wedding present. Still, fans might say, Mum's marriage was her own affair and they were more worried about Cliff's activities. With his increasing Christian commitments and talk of giving up show business for the classroom and becoming teacher Cliff or, perhaps, plain Mr H. Webb, there seemed cause for real concern. By October the flow of letters and cards had become a flood. That month it was reported that he had received pleading letters from an estimated 10,000. He received a forty-yard-long petition which had been organized by eighteen-year-old secretary Mary Clifford. She had taken out advertisements in major music papers all over the world. Cliff promised he would think seriously about it and expressed how pleased he was by such loyalty.

For the general public it was Cliff's stage appearance at Earls Court, London, on 16 June with Dr Billy Graham, a persuasive, good-looking American evangelist, which set the alarm bells ringing. Cliff sang 'It's No Secret' as a testimony song to his new faith and spoke inside Earls Court to 25,000, later going outside and speaking to thousands who could not get in. The next morning the British press, especially the tabloids, told the story and parents across the nation tried desperately to comfort their upset offspring. Many believed he could not continue as a pop star and certainly some Christians felt this was definitely a decision he must make.

The worries of his fans were increased when it was announced that his fan club would cease activity, but some said the reason lay elsewhere for it was becoming increasingly difficult to run the affairs of the club now that there were over 40,000 members scattered all over the world.

Reports of Cliff's withdrawal from show business continued unabated, but in one of his rare comments to the press Cliff's manager discounted these

1966

Opposite above: With their duplicates on the *Thunderbirds* set

Opposite below: What guy wouldn't look happy dancing with Viviane Ventura? Here, it's part of filming for *Finders Keepers*, June 1966

rumours and said Cliff was studying in the evenings but he had contractual commitments for some time ahead.

By July, Cliff and The Shadows were filming *Finders Keepers*. So at least whatever happened in the future the fans would have something to look forward to at the end of the year.

Finders Keepers had Cliff and The Shadows, Graham Stark, Robert Morley, Peggy Mount and delicious looking Viviane Ventura in its line-up. It was an Inter-State Films production for United Artists. Cliff and The Shadows played a group who find themselves with a hotel booking but then later, to their consternation, learn that the management cannot pay them. They form a friendship with local people and they hear how a traditional fiesta is threatened by a clutch of bombs which has been dropped by accident from an American aircraft. Cliff played himself. The Shadows provided the music.

The film was shot at Pinewood Studios and it was to this legendary film location that the press came and sought further news of Cliff's future career. They were singularly uninterested in the film, but at least for Christian Cliff and those in sympathy with his views the journalists' interest meant that Christian sentiments permeated the show-biz sections of the daily newspapers. And reporters did accept, and said so in their copy, the integrity of his beliefs. They did not feel that it was a publicity stunt (and why should he need one, anyway?) and were conscious that he felt it was his duty to spread the good news of Christian faith.

Cliff told how he set time aside for Bible reading and prayer and said that he did not think sex outside marriage was a good thing, that more than moderate drinking of alcohol was not recommended, and that he was against alcoholic spirits. He thought he wasn't clever enough to get a degree but he felt four more O-levels (he had obtained an O-level in religious education during the year) were possible and a teaching diploma eventually. He talked of his riches and thought he could live on £20 a week if he had to. The press commented that he had two cars – an MG and an E-type Jaguar – while one writer told of

1966

how he met Cliff carrying an evening dress shirt which cost £15.10s. It was obvious the press would concentrate on Cliff's lifestyle. Another writer said the star had eighteen suits, had bought houses for his family and himself, and had a villa in Portugal. Certainly during the months ahead Cliff would suffer endless interviews which would probe and probe.

Cliff had begun speaking to groups about his faith and had in fact made his debut as far back as January when he gave a talk on Christian maturity at Lewes in Sussex. On that occasion, he confessed, he had been terrified. He had been very nervous at Earls Court on the night of 16 June also.

At least one of Cliff's enduring attractions – his ability to be normal and natural – was unchanged by his new commitment. He was not a self-righteous type of person yet he made clear what he did and did not believe. And even if he came out with a rather heavy line or two they seemed, from his lips at any rate, to lack pomposity.

'I fight evil. If I think rotten things I hate myself. I try to be fair to people. Sometimes it is hard,' he said on one occasion. And as to working hard at being Cliff Richard, the answer to that suggestion was a firm: 'No, I don't work everything out as people sometimes think I do.' Cliff told reporters that the driving force which had made him Cliff Richard, Pop Star, was simple: 'I wanted to sing, that is all.' What was unexpected lay in the way in which his career had widened.

At Pinewood he said: 'I never imagined all this,' as he surveyed the trappings of filmland, but as with acting in general he had one straightforward aim: 'I've wanted to do everything properly and make a success of it.'

Certainly he felt that films were the nearest he had ever got to glamour and he had been amazed at all the fuss and bother and the attention to detail which went into making movies.

On 8 December *Finders Keepers* had its premiere at the Odeon, Leicester Square, London, with Cliff causing the usual ripple of excitement by escorting a young lady (this time it was Pippa Steel, a member of the *Cinderella* cast, his pantomime of 1966).

So Cliff returned to the screen after a gap of two years. United Artists in their press release for the film said the reason for the gap was simple – the right script hadn't come his way. Now it had.

Cliff's other film of the year was *Thunderbirds Are Go* where a puppet depicted what was called the 'Junior Cliff' and The Shadows were each depicted in similar fashion. *Thunderbirds Are Go* was a very successful TV puppet series of the time, the creation of highly inventive Gerry and Sylvia Anderson. It was made into a full length movie for the wide screen in the UK with costs reckoned in the region of £200,000. It was filmed in technicolour and employed stereophonic sound, with two units spending seven months making it.

In October the *Sunday Mirror* told of Cliff's invitation to tour Eastern bloc countries. He was due for concerts in Russia, Czechoslovakia, Bulgaria and Yugoslavia, but Russia never became a reality until after the mid-1970s. During 1966 Cliff visited Portugal (for a holiday at his villa) and that was all the travelling he did. In terms of some

previous years it was a rather homebound year for him. But apart from Mum's marriage, a film, and the sale of his house, there was a BBC TV special (the first for three years) in March and *Cinderella*, his Christmas pantomime, to occupy him. The beginning of the year had also seen his entry into cabaret which took place at London's famed Talk of the Town. It began at the end of January and ran through February and was an obvious play at the older market. It proved highly successful.

The year 1966 began and ended with Cliff still a pop star in spite of rumours and reported statements supposedly made by Cliff to the contrary. It also gave him his O-level pass in religious education. Of the day when he sat the exam at a grammar school in Sussex he says: 'Every so often a teacher poked his head round the door to make sure I wasn't cheating. I wasn't and I passed!'

Cliff, looking back on 1966, says the continuous speculation as to what he might or might not do proved embarrassing and pressurized his own thinking. He sees some earlier statements of his as rather premature

and hasty and when he decided he would stay in music some people reacted by saying he was staying because of the money. Cliff says it was really a case of seeing how God could use him, as a Christian, in show business. And certainly Cliff the pop star and Christian has led to Gospel albums, major religious meetings, radio and television 'witness' appearances. If he had become a religious education teacher none of these major areas of evangelism would have been his. Some 'religious' people opposed his staying in show business and they criticize him for it to this day. They seem blinkered and even blind to its evangelistic possibilities.

Music fans, however, still felt uncertain about Cliff's future.

Opposite: Geoffrey Everitt, first post-war DJ and manager of Radio Luxembourg, hands our man a special award

Above: Just a little unsure of the steps – rehearsing for *Cinderella*

Following pages: Australia goes mad over Cliff and The Shadows

Was he or wasn't he leaving show business was the question of 1966, and if it had seemed more or less certain by the end of the year that he would stay, the uncertainty started up again almost at the start of 1967.

Cliff debated and argued with himself, asked for advice and prayed. One moment he was saying: 'I must get out of show business as soon as possible. But how do I do it?' The next, he was stating: 'I've found I can mix both my Christian life and my show-biz life because I treat my show-biz life as we are Biblically told, as a job we're going to give to God.'

It made everyone, particularly his fans, uneasy and it suggested the eventual separation of Cliff and The Shadows. Certainly, The Shadows seemed to be drifting more and more into their own solo work. Nonetheless, whatever the state of Cliff's mind and heart, the record hits still came. There were four chart singles, two EPs and three albums, including the first of what was to become a fairly regular stream of Gospel material, the album *Good News*.

'The trouble is,' said Cliff at this time, 'I never seem to age. I've had my hair flicked up in an effort to make me look older but it doesn't work. It just makes me look different.' Oddly enough, fifteen years later in 1982 he was trying, not for the first time, to grow a beard and he was photographed with a few days of stubble and hair (for Cliff) somewhat awry. He commented: 'I still look like a fourteen-year-old trying to look forty. It's embarrassing really.' And at the beginning of 1967 it was revealed that his O-level, Oxford GCE pass in religious education had been grade 3. Another hangover from 1966 was the pantomime *Cinderella*, with Cliff commenting: 'I'm not bored with doing it night after night. Every show is different. Audiences are different – some are hard, some aren't.'

He told young people at Cuffley Free Church in Hertfordshire: 'Pre-marital sex is unhealthy to the mind.' He told teenagers on another of his *Five to Ten* broadcasts for the BBC's Light Programme that it was bad for them to hear suggestive lyrics in pop songs.

In a newspaper article he commented on Mick Jagger's

Below: Apparently about to be strangled by a tarantula, but still smiling through

Opposite above: Make-up time for the TV cameras. Brian is front far right, Bruce behind him

Opposite below: To kiss or not to kiss – Sandi Shaw obviously hopes for the former!

announcement that he would live with Marianne Faithfull without being married to her. Cliff said it was Jagger's own affair but he would not contemplate doing that himself.

He was scathing about people – famous ones especially – who thought LSD was good. Cliff said: 'You don't find Christians drugging around and sleeping around because we have a set of rules that keeps us stable.' Cliff appealed to pop stars to use their influence responsibly.

At the same time he was angry with those who labelled him 'Vicar Richard' and 'The High Priest of Pop'. He said: 'A lot of people think this is a big gimmick. That I'm not sincere about it. Well, I am.'

At least he found sympathy from Ray Connolly, who said: 'He's no fanatic. He is, however, so deeply concerned with his religion that any conversation tends to drift back to that overriding influence in his life.'

Cliff admitted to Ray the possibility of his once being a sex symbol, but added: 'I wouldn't like to think that the majority of girls who follow me are thinking about leaping into bed with me.' He said he was upset by the permissive society and he wished he had found his religious faith many years previously: 'I would have matured mentally much more quickly. I don't mind if I get laughed at now and again. If I'd been born 2,000 years ago I'd have been thrown to the lions. I think I'd rather be laughed at.'

Speculation about Cliff's future continued, fuelled by his own indecision. In April he told the *New Musical Express* that he had never thought of becoming a clergyman. He said he wouldn't be up to it. Later in the same month, he told readers of *Disc and Music Echo* he was terminating his career as soon as he possibly could: 'Ideally I'd like to start teaching religious instruction in 1968.' He said he would keep the 'Cliff' part of his name but not the Richard. It would be plain Mr C. Webb for the staffroom notice board. But on another occasion he said he hadn't changed his mind about retiring one day to teach religion but it might be as much as ten years away.

This year also saw the publication of the first full-length biography of Cliff, written by journalist David

1967

Winter under the title *The Cliff Richard Story: New Singer, New Song*. The book was launched, with two others, at Church House, Westminster. Dr Donald Coggan, Archbishop of York, whose own book *Prayers of the New Testament* was one of the other two, attended the launch, as did Cliff.

In April the *Daily Mirror* announced: 'It's All Over – Cliff and The Shadows part'. In reality The Shadows were to spend May and June on a ten-week tour of the world and in the meantime Cliff would be filming without them. Later in the summer, 4-6 August, The Shadows appeared at the first national song festival in Yugoslavia. Although the days of Cliff and The Shadows were numbered, at the year's end they would appear in the Christmas Day television presentation of *Aladdin*.

In the spring, news of Cliff's next film, *Two a Penny*, was announced, as was the fact that he would represent Britain in the 1968 Eurovision Song Contest. He would sing selected songs in an initial British contest and the winning number from these would be the one he would sing at the final.

He began filming in May, with finance for the picture coming from Worldwide Films, Burbank, California, part of the Billy Graham Evangelistic Organization. Cliff found himself in trouble when he announced that he would film for nothing. The actors' union, Equity, protested and Cliff was forced to accept the minimum payment of £40. Cliff gave the money to charity. Dora Bryan, Ann Holloway, Avil Angers and Nigel Goodwin were in the cast of fifteen. Billy Graham played himself. Nigel Goodwin became an influential friend and Christian pastor to Cliff and was heavily involved in the Arts Centre Group.

The film music was composed and conducted by Mike Leander and the original story and screenplay was by Stella Linden. Cliff was cast as Jamie Hopkins, a drug pedlar who is introduced to Christianity by his girlfriend Carol. At the film's end Jamie is undecided about Christianity and the viewer is left to decide whether he becomes a follower. However, right at the end of the film Cliff appears as himself in a recording studio. He says Jamie was someone who started looking for answers. Cliff himself had found the answer.

Many were disappointed that the film failed to achieve major cinema showing in the UK although in some respects this was not surprising since it was clearly an evangelistic film.

Cliff wrote three songs for the film: 'Questions', 'Love You Forever Today', and the title song 'Two a Penny'. The first two were co-written with J.F. Collier. The premiere took place at the Prince Charles Theatre, London, on 20 June 1968.

Other events in 1967 included Cliff's appearances in July on TV with Dr Graham for the ABC programme *Looking For an Answer* and again later on the same show with a sceptical Paul Jones (of Manfred Mann).

Cliff had his usual holiday in Portugal, though only three weeks this time. He was voted the Best Dressed Male Star by readers of music weekly *Disc and Music Echo*, won the Top Male Singer award in *Melody Maker*, told the Beatles they were wasting their time with the Maharishi for the answer was in Jesus Christ, said he would love to play Heathcliff in *Wuthering Heights*, performed in Tokyo with a Japanese orchestra (14 October), and in December landed a role as a straight actor in the TV thriller *A Matter of Diamonds*. He was cast as a young man who decides to rob a girl but finds himself falling in love with her. He was also one of ten people featured in a book called *Ten of Our Time* by Joan Clifford which appeared in 1967. It told, albeit briefly, the highlights of his career and why it was he had decided he would become a Christian. And not unexpectedly the text asked the by now familiar question, 'Is he or isn't he going to retire?' The question was still around in 1968!

1967

Learning Czech for the Bratislava Song Contest

1968

'Congratulations' was the winning song for the British entry to the Eurovision Song Contest and Cliff sang it on the *Cilla Black Show* on Tuesday, 12 March. The record sold over a million and gave Cliff his fifth gold disc. As well as being a British number one it topped the German charts for seven weeks.

Some 200,000,000 people watched the contest which was held at London's Royal Albert Hall on 6 April. It was a cliff-hanger with Britain and Spain running neck and neck. And there was a delightful mix-up at the end when Yugoslavia gave the UK eleven marks when the maximum was ten! When the correction had been made the result was clear – Spain 29, Britain 28. 'La, La, La' had won for vocalist Massiel. Cliff said he was disappointed, but his record sold in far greater numbers than the winning song. He excited gossip journalists by describing the Spanish singer Maria de Los Angeles Santamaria (Massiel) as a 'bombshell' (Maria was a last-minute replacement for Juan Manuel Serrat who had said he wouldn't sing the song in Castilian Spanish, the national language).

April 1968 saw more than the Eurovision Song Contest. The sad, though expected, announcement was made that Cliff and The Shadows were splitting. The *Mirror* on 18 April confirmed that Cliff was breaking away from Hank, Bruce, Brian and John. Journalist Don Short said: 'It's the end of an era. And there will be a lot of sighs, a lot of tears to wipe away from fretting fans across the world. But it had to happen one day.'

Cliff's new-found faith was largely responsible for it was taking an increasing amount of his time. Bruce Welch said: 'Cliff is very sincere about his faith and we would not dream of interfering. We admire him, in fact, tremendously.' The Palladium show on 14 December was named as The Shadows' farewell date although there was speculation about further joint records. On 19 September Cliff and The Shadows opened an extraordinarily long twelve-and-a-half-week season at the Palladium though in fact The Shadows joined Cliff from the beginning of October after their Danish tour had been completed. Previous to this the Chris Barber Band were on the Cliff bill.

In September also Cliff celebrated his tenth anniversary in show business and they were all together at a special party held in London's West End. Interviews were conducted in different parts of the room and in one The Shadows said: 'We are through.' Cliff at the other end commented: 'It has been a lot of fun working together, but it is time for us all to make a change. You cannot go on doing the same things for ever.'

The Shadows recalled the early days when they worked out what became known as the 'cross-over step' and learnt the famed routine of holding their guitars at certain angles and turning at the same moment so that a particular phrase was emphasized. At first The Shadows saw themselves as a backing group but then when their own success came they set their sights higher. They told of how they had found Cliff to be modest, a rather retiring person. And as they put it: 'There have been many eventful moments whilst we have been Shadowing Cliff.'

There was of course much other activity during the year. The International Cliff Richard Fan Club had sprung up in Amsterdam and was to grow in strength, lasting into the 1980s with increased vigour and scope. The club aimed at an initial 1,000 members from Britain and it already had 1,500 Dutch members.

At the Bratislava Song Festival in Czechoslovakia on 13–16 June Cliff fell ill and The Shadows substituted. *Two a Penny* was premiered at London's Prince Charles Theatre on June 20. David Winter's biography of

Cliff went into its deserved third edition and Winter's coverage received this comment from Kenneth Allsop: 'With a candid twinkle in his eye Mr Winter pulls no punches. He doesn't want to give the impression that Cliff is an unctuous prig.' Other Cliff books selling well were *The Way I See It* by Cliff and the film story of *Two a Penny*.

Cliff had his own one-man TV show for the BBC on 28 June entitled *Cliff Richard at The Talk of the Town* which brought to everyone's table the four-week act Cliff had begun on 13 May at the famed London nightspot. And on the independent channel there was a TV special on 11 June with Cliff Richard and The Shadows to celebrate the year of their tenth anniversary. He also appeared on ITV's *Big Show* and sang 'The Day I Met Marie', 'All My Love' and 'Shout'. On a BBC show on 28 June he sang 'Shout', 'All My Love', 'Nothing But a Houseparty', 'If Ever I Should Leave You' (from *Camelot*),

'Girl', 'London's Not Too Far', 'The Day I Met Marie', 'The Dreams I Dream', 'The Lady Came from Baltimore', a medley of his hits, the Beatle song 'When I'm Sixty-four', 'Congratulations', part of 'Visions', and he played guitar on 'A Taste of Honey'. Vocal backing was given by The Breakaways.

He spent six weeks in the United States in August and early September with manager Peter Gormley. Back in Britain he played Stockton's Fiesta on 9 September, the first cabaret for Cliff outside London.

Cliff's twenty-year-old sister Jackie married nineteen-year-old landscape gardener Peter Harrison at Hoddesdon Register Office on 14 September when Cliff's Mum delighted the press by saying: 'All I have to do now is get Cliff married off.' Cliff was not being drawn on prospects in this direction. He was more forthcoming on the now classic question 'Is he or isn't he?' replying that he was not. 'I know a lot of people will knock me and claim I've sacrificed principles for money but I haven't changed. I'm still a Christian.' He said his role in the Billy Graham Organization's *Two a Penny* made him realize he could be an active Christian in show business.

There were also of course Cliff's religious activities. He gave Continental concerts with The Settlers and appeared with them at Coventry Cathedral on 22 September and future dates in January 1969 were announced. On 1 December Cliff and The Settlers featured in Manchester's Holy Trinity Church in the BBC 1 series *Songs of Praise*. He took part in the Christmas cake cutting for the Mental Health Trust at the Carlton Tower Hotel, London, on 4 December.

In the 1968 *NME* poll Cliff was voted number one British Vocal Personality, number one British Male Singer and number three World Male Singer with Elvis and Tom Jones occupying the first and second places

Famed photographer Dezo Hoffmann explains to Cliff the kind of pic he would like to shoot

1968

respectively. The Shadows easily won the British Instrumental unit section. 'Congratulations' was voted Britain's fourth best disc of the year, while according to the year's chart positions Cliff was twenty-second.

EMI issued four singles, no EPs (and there would be no future releases in this style until a three-track 45 rpm with Olivia Newton-John in 1971) and three albums – *Cliff in Japan, Two a Penny* and *Established 1958.*

On a more gossipy level, the press and fans learnt that Cliff was taking speech and drama lessons with the aim of broadening his scope, he bought himself a Volvo E-Type Jaguar, again went boating on the Norfolk Broads, spent time at his Portuguese villa, and was seen to have slimmed. When he and The Shadows gave their tenth anniversary party one newspaper was moved to say it had none of the expected Tin Pan Alley pop image for there was no long hair and no deafening-sound-and-blue-smoke atmosphere but rather a collection of well-dressed and pleasant people. It was reported that Cliff had owned fifteen cars, had only had half a dozen piano lessons in his life and earned £50,000 plus a year.

On a more serious level, on 1 April ATV showed the play *A Matter of Diamonds* (the night after he had appeared on the *Morecombe and Wise Show*) and Cliff said it was a television role which 'I am taking seriously'. It co-starred Hollywood lady Evelyn Keyes. 'Acting in *A Matter of Diamonds* is just the opportunity I've been waiting for to add a completely new and fascinating dimension to my career,' said Cliff.

Questions and debate still followed Cliff and his appearances in South Africa, with the press having denounced his past statement that he hadn't noticed apartheid in that country. Cliff did point out that he had insisted on shows for white and coloured people and said: 'If they are childish enough not to let them sit next to each other then that's their problem, and they'll get over it. It's a young country.'

He said the people of Africa knew he didn't agree with apartheid and added: 'As long as I don't go there with them thinking I support apartheid I can't be said to be supporting it, can I? But if they want me to go and sing . . . I'll go and sing to them.'

So 1968 passed with endless radio, TV and press activity, and much unacknowledged activity. He had been for instance with Keith Skues on *Saturday Club* (2 October), been interviewed for the Voice of Germany and Australian radio, done a special interview for the huge-selling girls' weekly *Jackie*, appeared on *Pop Inn*, and been photographed by Dezo Hoffmann for a Dental Council promotion! He had appeared on David Jacobs' radio show, performed at the yearly *NME* concert (12 May), been a panel member of *Any Questions* on BBC Radio (22 May), appeared on Spanish TV, chosen his eight favourite discs for *Off the Record*, made a tape for the Pakistan section of the BBC, recorded in Germany, made a five-minute tape for the blind, filmed for German TV, been interviewed for the Canadian Broadcasting Corporation and by Adrian Love for the BBC World Service. He had appeared on the top-ranking *Dee Time* on 14 December and on 27 December he departed by flight BE 218 for Malta, returning New Year's Day 1969.

This had been the pattern for years, albeit hidden from the general public in its extent and all backed up with endless days in rehearsal. And now in addition he was speaking at Christian meetings, many of them humble affairs in churches and schools. He must have been exhausted.

The year 1968 was important but 1969 promised to be even more critical for Cliff. It was the last year of a decade and would see him into the seventies. Could he keep both show business and Christian activities flourishing? Could he retain his health? Could he maintain public affection without the lovable Shadows? The year 1969 held the answers.

1968

Taken at the Simon Dee BBC TV show in 1968

With Cilla Black in his TV show on 17 May. Together they produced something special

In the last year of the 1960s Cliff had four singles and two albums released and celebrated his twenty-ninth birthday. It was a year without real controversy. He survived on his own but in the autumn The Shadows were back with Hank Marvin, Brian Bennett, John Rostill, and Alan Hawkshaw for Bruce Welch. They spent a fortnight in Japan with Cliff and then toured Britain with him.

Cliff was in Britain on 1 January, arriving back from Malta at 19.35 on flight BE 185. By 2 January he was busy in rehearsal for a six-part Gospel series for Tyne Tees TV entitled *Life With Johnny*. He was also hard at work on a Scottish colour TV show called *Cliff in Scotland*. Along with Cliff in the Tyne Tees series were The Settlers with their striking lead lady Cindy Kent from Birmingham.

Tyne Tees rehearsals took up most of January and the beginning of February. Then he began rehearsal for the Cilla Black BBC TV show. He was kept busy in 1969 by television. During his February–March visit to Europe he appeared on the German show *The Golden Shot* and sang 'Don't Forget to Catch Me' in German. In the first week of March he was guest star in the Rumania song contest in Brasnov. In Holland he sang three songs on the TV show *Waauw* – 'Don't Forget to Catch Me', 'The Day I Met Marie' and 'Good Times'. He had his own BBC 1 show on 17 May and a few days later he was off on flight BA 760 to Hollywood.

His guests on the BBC 1 show were Hank Marvin, Una Stubbs, Sheila White and The Breakaways. Cliff opened the show with 'My Babe', moved to 'Congratulations' and 'It's All in the Game'. Hank had a solo turn with 'A Place in the Sun' and then sang 'Feeling Groovy' with Cliff.

Cliff was the noble lover in a brief skit on *Saturday Playhouse* and later sang 'The Minute You're Gone', 'Take a Bird Who Can Sing', 'The Day I Met Marie', his latest single 'Big Ship', and 'Visions' among other items. There was also a skit on John and Yoko's extended stay in bed to promote peace when Cliff and Hank sang the old English song 'Oh No John, No John, No'. Other media appearances for Cliff included several on *Sooty*, the *Dave Cash Radio One Show* (26 March), *Top of the Pops* (21 February and 4 April) and BBC *Radio*

1969

One Club (18 February and 15 April). He appeared, yet again, at the *NME* Poll Concert and for the thousands attending he sang 'Move It', 'Good Times Better Times', 'The Day I Met Marie', 'La La La La La La' and 'Congratulations'. Hank played 'Goodnight Dick' and 'Laura's Theme'.

Autumn was busy. On 15–20 September he made a return to the Fiesta Club in Stockton. Stories circulated about his payment but one fairly well substantiated figure suggested he was paid £5,000 for the week. All tickets were sold. He had a sixteen-piece band with Brian, John and Alan of The Shadows amongst them, as well as The Cookies. The songs were all familiar; the set length was ninety minutes.

In October he was in Japan for concerts in Tokyo, Osaka, Kyoto and Nagoya. Japan issued 'Shi Awasa-No-Asa', which in English means 'Early in the Morning'.

On 5 November he began his British tour but had to cancel the last date, at Manchester on the 15th, because of sickness. His show at Croydon on 6 November was attended by the London music press. Everyone heard the old standards and if Cliff had now become a very polished performer there were definite reminders of former times as girls danced in the aisles and the stage was showered with love gifts. The Cookies, a four-girl singing group from Australia, had begun the show and there was also the re-formed Shadows with keyboard effects from organist-pianist Alan Hawkshaw, but still with their old popular sound.

After his British tour ended Cliff was busy rehearsing with The Settlers, fitting in some Christian work at Ballards Lane Methodist Church, Finchley, London, before flying to Norway on 23 November, a day after The Settlers had departed for the same country. On the 28th he was singing 'Throw Down the Line' and 'Eyes of a Child' for a Paris TV station.

In December there was another religious booking at the City of London School. On 8 December he recorded *Christmas With Cliff* for the BBC with a host of interviews for various radio stations following. On the 10th he attended a charity show at the Palladium, for the Royal Society

for the Prevention of Cruelty to Animals. He visited 10 Downing Street on the 11th and did a charity show at the Café Royal on the 12th. Life was very busy. He was also filming for Cilla Black's Christmas Eve TV show, visited his old school for a dinner on the 17th and appeared on a 1960s TV special a day later.

Cliff appeared at the Odeon in Manchester on 20 December and before Christmas had run its course he was already recording new material and busy in the TV studios.

Other happenings included news of another book by Cliff, called *Questions*, scheduled for publication in February 1970. There was a special Newcastle Gospel charity concert from Cliff and The Settlers on 28 March. The Billy Graham Organization said they could not find any circuit which would take *Two a Penny* but various cinemas in major towns had asked for it. A riot almost broke out when it was at first thought that the Tyne Tees TV Gospel series with Cliff and Cindy Kent would not be taken by London's Thames TV and petitions were hurriedly organized to reverse this decision. Denmark took the *Cliff in Scotland* TV show.

One newspaper carried the headline 'Cliff Richard Told Me' and underneath quoted Cliff saying: '"I was chatting with some friends the other day and Paul said . . . " '"Paul?" I asked. '"You know, Paul the Apostle; I was quoting him," explained Cliff as casually as if he were introducing an old friend.'

Cliff told of the BBC chasing him for a series but he said he was trying to work out something a little different and said he didn't want the usual TV format. He pleaded for some good film scripts in which he would not be just a larger-than-life Cliff Richard. He said: 'I want a tiny little nothing part opposite Albert Finney or someone, that demands real acting – being someone else other than CR. No one takes me seriously. I have an unfortunate image.' He told journalists that he couldn't buy a Rolls because his conscience wouldn't permit him to spend so much, but then he did buy a Jensen. He explained it was important he should travel in comfort and so arrive at a concert fresh and at ease. He talked of fishing in Portugal and how he had

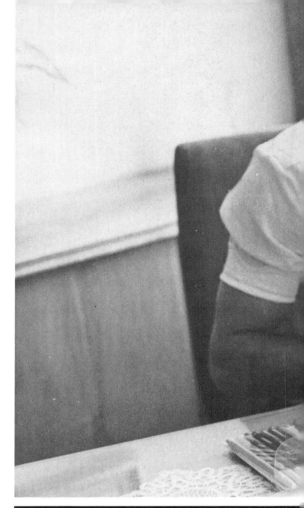

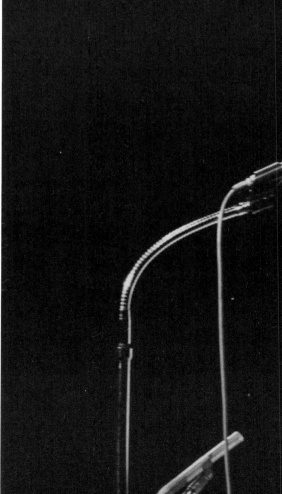

found that melon skins attract fish. 'If I know I'm going fishing I always make sure melon is on the lunch menu!' He was wearing fairly sober suits at this time but liked flashy shirts and said he bought his suits at Mr Fish of Savile Row where they were '£75 a touch but you get an exclusive design'.

Roderick Mann of the *Sunday Express* said there was something wholesome about CR – he would make the ideal breakfast food. But he said Cliff made a nice change from 'those long-haired singing scruffs'. He remarked how Cliff had never been involved in a scandal, run off with a tycoon's daughter or done anything vaguely beastly. Mann said: 'No wonder he is every mother's dream son.'

Cliff told women's journalist Jane Reid: 'Even if I don't marry before thirty-two, I shan't worry too much.'

He said that when all The Shadows began the marriage trail he felt worried and left behind but now at the end of the 1960s it didn't bother him. His mind was on the seventies.

1969

Above: Autographs, autographs and autographs . . . with love

Left: Showing his winning artistry on a TV recording, 1969

Right: Recording in Lisbon

Below: Still in Lisbon, with David Bryce in the centre foreground

Opposite: At last some time to relax – sitting on a boat near his holiday villa in Portugal

Right: Spain – a steady hand and a good aim is what it takes

Below: Seriously folks, we're pretty good. Cliff, Bruce and Hank

Bottom: Supposedly looking down at a church spire in Munich but distracted

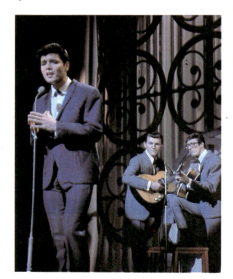

Below: In Bremen with The Shadows on their first German tour

Bottom: They know, and the audience agrees, that it's been a great show. Cliff, Una Stubbs and The Shadows in an Aladdin curtain call

Right: Cliff bemused by a novel Easter present

Below: Storytelling time for the kids in the studio and those at home watching television

Bottom: November 1973, a clothes fitting at Berman's in London

Left: At home, looking for the lost chord

Below: Feeding time in Australia and hopefully fingers are not included in the giraffe's idea of high living

At the Royal Albert Hall, London, 1982

Left: It's written loud and clear — he loves performing. The Royal Albert Hall, 1982

Below: His bedroom at Toronto's Hotel Chelsea Delta, 1981

Bottom: David Bryce's lights shown at their best for Cliff on stage at Sunbury, Ontario, Canada

Well, if the qualified surgeon isn't around I'll just have to do it and hope the patient doesn't know

Opposite: Cliff committed 100 per cent and for twenty-five years as well!

Opposite above: Letting loose during his season at The Talk of the Town, London

Opposite below: Surgeon Cliff again – a scene from his BBC1 series early in the year

1970

Cliff had made hit records and filled halls across the world. TV and radio programmes had been plentiful. There had been cabaret and pantomime, films both serious and amusing. But at this point in his career one major ambition remained, and 1970 saw it realized.

Cliff had a burning desire to make his mark as a straight actor. May saw him find an opportunity to realize this ambition when he joined the cast of *Five Finger Exercise* at Bromley New Theatre.

'This is something I have wanted to do for a long time. For five years I've dropped hints but when you're a pop singer no one wants to take you seriously. Acting is almost the only thing I haven't tried. Perhaps I shall prove conclusively that I'm only a pop singer.

'I'm not looking for great reviews, don't get me wrong. Of course I like good notices but it wouldn't upset me if the critics said I was lousy, they wouldn't put me off. I'm here to learn. I could have gone on doing the easy things but you have to expand and pick up the challenge.'

His Bromley challenge ate savagely into his time schedules. On 21 April he began a hectic three weeks of rehearsal and on 11 May the play opened.

An unexpected aspect of the newspaper coverage was the story of how his trousers kept splitting. The 81-year-old wardrobe mistress said he always wore his trousers too tight. She commented: 'I took them home to mend but the next day the same thing happened. Then I realized he was wearing them so tight that I had to ask the stage manager for some of her jeans to put some material into his trousers!'

The reviews were fairly good. Cliff had triumphed again! And for the occasion he grew a beard. 'I tried to convince the audience I was not just another pop star trying to act.' The producer had other ideas, for he thought the beard made Cliff look too old for his role, so off it came.

Much more happened in 1970 than *Five Finger Exercise* but this was most certainly the personal highlight of the year for Cliff.

There were of course recording sessions as well and 1970 saw the issue of three singles and no less than four albums. There were also concerts across the world.

Two of the albums were religious. *About That Man* featured Cliff telling the story of Jesus utilizing the basic framework of the Living New Testament translation. *His Land* was the soundtrack from the second film released in March, that he made with and for the Billy Graham Evangelistic Organization, the filming having been done during the previous year in Israel.

As for concerts, Cliff spent a week beginning 6 April at Batley Variety Club (The Shadows were in residence the following week!). It was announced in the spring that Cliff would play London's Talk of the Town for four weeks in October. The Shadows would not be backing him.

Early in June he was preparing for an overseas tour. On the 10th he was

off to Austria on flight BE 700. He made concert appearances in Rumania and Czechoslovakia on the 11th, 12th and 13th and once more attended the Bratislava Song Festival. During his time on the Continent he filmed for German TV in Berlin on the 18th and 19th. Not long after returning from Cologne on 20 June he was planning his new South African tour for which he departed on 3 July. In Natal he addressed a special meeting at the request of the Bishop.

While he was in South Africa it was confirmed that he would play at the Talk of the Town between 28 September and 24 October. He would also, along with The Shadows, tour the UK on 11–14 and 18–21 November. A booking was announced for German TV on 15 March 1971 under the title *Cliff in Berlin*.

Radio and TV dates during 1970 included the *Dave Cash Show* once more, BBC's Disney TV film show *Children's Favourites*, *Top of the Pops*, Radio 1 with Stuart Grundy, filming over six days for a BBC TV special, *The Cliff Richard Show*, and recording for BBC Radio One's *Sing a New Song*. On the religious side he recorded a number of Scripture readings for the BBC.

He also made charity appearances of various kinds. On 8 February he was at the Leicester Youth Show, and on 23 March he gave a picture session for the National Association of Youth Clubs. He also did a photo session for the *Girl Guide Annual* on 13 April. There were a number of church and youth club gatherings, among them the East London Youth Club on 8 June, Hatfield School on 10 October, the London Methodist Society on 18 October, and a rally in Belfast on 7 November.

And he was house hunting. A number of days in October and November were earmarked for the task in his diary. Cliff finally settled on a splendid house in Weybridge. It was owned by actress Anita Richardson and her husband, building contractor Edward Biddle. They said they had an enquiry from a Mr Harry Webb! 'I recognized him the moment I opened the door but he was very nice and friendly though I wondered if the house was a bit large for him because he was not married.' The couple were asking for around £40,000.

1970

Cliff received his usual assortment of awards during the year including, early in 1970, *Disc and Music Echo*'s Valentine's Day Award. He was voted Mr Valentine. He was voted the Best Dressed Star, came second in the Top British Singer category and his *Sincerely Cliff* was voted the sixth most popular album by the paper's readers. The Songwriters' Guild of Great Britain gave him an award for being the singer who had given the most exemplary service to British music during the preceding year.

In October Mary Whitehouse's National Viewers' and Listeners' Association presented him with their annual award for his 'outstanding contribution to religious broadcasting and light entertainment'. Mrs Whitehouse told him he had made nonsense of the so-called 'generation gap'. *Record Mirror* voted him Top British Male Singer.

He spent 30 July to 11 August on the Broads with Christian friends. Soon after he was back he attended a press reception for his album *About That Man*.

At the Talk of the Town in September/October Cliff, backed by The Cookies with Brian Bennett on drums, sang many of his hits, did a rock 'n' roll medley including 'Jailhouse Rock' and 'Great Balls of Fire', and played some acoustic guitar for 'I Who Have Nothing'. General material went right back in time and included 'Move It' and 'Living Doll'. On 10 October he was presented with letters, poems, photographs and birthday cards from fans in South-East Asia.

The autumn tour kicked off in Newcastle on 13 November. The Johnny Wiltshire sound opened and Brian Bennett conducted amidst his drum kit. The show also featured the Marvin-Farrar partnership. Cliff came on for the second half. He talked about his Christian faith and about some of the ridicule which had come his way. He sang, among other songs, the Bacharach numbers 'The Look of Love' and 'Walk On By', plus oldies and the rock 'n' roll medley which had been part of his set at the Talk of the Town. The last number, 'I Saw the Light', really set the place humming.

During the year three US labels – Warners, Monument and World – had material of his on the market.

Sadly the planned *Life With Johnny* series album was cancelled though titles were printed by the ever informative *Dynamite* magazine.

He had a TV special for BBC and Scandinavian TV jointly on Christmas Eve and early in the year his new book *Questions* had gone on sale for 5s. Radio One and Two ran *The Cliff Richard Story* with Robin Boyle.

It had been a busy year as usual and a good start to the 1970s.

Above: Watching the World Cup – England *v.* Czechoslovakia – with David Bryce far right, in a private house in Bratislava

Opposite: Fun time for Una, Cliff and Hank

1970

1971

Cliff's three-month BBC TV series, *It's Cliff Richard*, was broadcast at the beginning of 1971, ending on 27 March. Hank alone and Hank with Marvin and Farrar guested on five of the programmes, while the year's British Eurovision singer, Mary Hopkin, sang her way through the songs from which one would be selected for the contest.

And while the fans had their joy, Cliff had his as well. He found himself another dramatic role, appearing in *The Potting Shed*. This should have run at Bromley New Theatre but due to a fire the venue was cancelled. The play did a quick transfer and opened a week late on 18 May at London's Sadlers Wells. Cliff's role – he played James Colliger – had been written for a 44-year-old and had been played by no less a person than Sir John Gielgud. For Cliff, Colliger became a thirty-year-old this time. Along with Cliff in the cast were Patrick Barr, Margot Thomas and Kathleen Harrison. The reviews commended Cliff.

Religion was very much on Cliff's mind during the year. He managed to find time for both sides of his career although of course religious themes permeated his show-business activities. Among the major events was an appearance before 5,000 young Methodists at the annual get-together of their youth movement at London's Royal Albert Hall on 16 May. Each year the afternoon and evening main displays have a special guest, and Cliff was one of them. He presented various sporting prizes and told of his Christian faith briefly. Arrangements were made so he could escape later from hordes of excited fans. The Methodist Association of Youth Clubs has a policy of keeping the name of their special guest a secret, so Cliff's arrival on stage was an occasion for hysterical acclaim.

He appeared on BBC radio's religious programme *Music for Sunday* presented by Dora Bryan and produced by Jack Davies. There were church conferences, evening meetings and youth group attendances,

Below: Maybe it's a birthday – they're toasting someone, anyway

Opposite: Tyne Tees TV series with The Settlers. Vivacious Cindy Kent is second from the left

including one at the famed All Souls, Langham Place, London, which is thronged with young people every Sunday morning, even in the 1980s. He helped out in the YMCA fund-raising walk, opened a fête at St Anthony's Hospital, Cheam, Surrey, spent some time at the Arts Centre Group and was part of a charity concert at the Palladium on 13 June. He also sang and talked at Coldinglay Prison, Surrey, was present at the Christian Film Awards ceremony, and appeared on stage for the Festival of Light at a meeting in Westminster Central Hall on 9 September. On 11 December he sang at a Christmas carol concert at London's Festival Hall. He also managed to see the musical *Godspell* and as usual (the sixth year running) he went carol singing around the streets of Finchley in North London at Christmas.

During 1971 he told top-selling girls' paper *Jackie* that he lived a normal and un-star-like existence. He helped run the church youth club, played badminton, was a regular church attender and enjoyed what he termed 'the Anglican way of worship'.

He told *Record Mirror* that

clairvoyancy and meddling with spirit forms were non-Christian. He said the Bible categorically forbade these things. They caused, he said, a great deal of mental disturbance: 'I know some people who have been physically harmed.' He was amused and saddened by the way the Christian faith was considered unfashionable in some quarters. 'People are funny. You can embrace Buddhism or meditate with the Maharishi, but talk of Christ and you embarrass them.' Cliff said Christmas was his favourite 'Christian' time. He loved the carols, the church ritual and the togetherness of family and friends.

Show-business Cliff marched on, though the chart performance of his singles was erratic, and none of his 1971 releases reached the top ten. He had no album releases this year. It was the beginning of a bad time for fans, and 1972 was to prove pretty bare as well, with just a *Best of Cliff Volume 2*. There was no new album until the soundtrack of *Take Me High* at the end of 1973!

However, 1971 saw another major European tour from 26 March to 9 April. The British tour kicked off on 17 November in Bristol with Marvin,

Welch and Farrar, plus the delicious Olivia Newton-John. It was a brief tour, ending on 4 December and interrupted by a Gospel concert, a religious gathering at Filey, and a Gospel rally at the Royal Albert Hall.

There were rumours of a film planned for 1971, but all in all it was not the brightest of years for Cliff's British followers once the BBC TV series had run its course. Things improved slightly at the end of the year when for three weeks Cliff, with Marvin, Welch and Farrar, and Olivia Newton-John and Dora Bryan, starred in the *Cliff Richard Show* at the London Palladium.

At the end of the year it was announced that he would make a film in 1973 and filming, at one time scheduled for September 1971, would take place in the spring of 1972. The tentative title was *Xanadu*. The film's location would be Newcastle-upon-Tyne.

The *NME* made a list of the thirty most successful artistes who had charted since 1956. Cliff was second with 9,700 points to Elvis' 12,844. Cliff also regained the *NME* poll award as Top British Male Singer. In

1971

Record Mirror's 1971 poll Cliff was number one male singer while Olivia Newton-John, who was managed by Cliff's expert Peter Gormley, won the top girl spot. Cliff found himself a pet dog and called her Kelly. At the eighth festival of the Rose d'Or at Antibes-Juan Les Pins in France on 5 July he and Olivia stole the show when they sang 'Don't Move Away'. Cliff received an Ivor Novello Award at the festival. He and Olivia appeared over three nights.

There was cabaret at Stockton's Fiesta Club on 13 September and also at the Fiesta, Sheffield, on 20–25 September. Dutch TV showed *One Day With Cliff Richard*, and it was announced that The New Seekers were to represent Britain in the 1972 Eurovision Song Contest. A selection of songs, one of which would be chosen as the British entry in the contest, would be featured over a number of weeks.

Another development in 1971 was that the British Cliff Richard Movement joined up with the International Cliff Richard Fan Club in Amsterdam and the new name was The International Cliff Richard Movement with headquarters in Amsterdam.

To fans eager to know if he was finally contemplating marriage, 31-year-old Cliff said his father didn't get married until he was thirty-two so 'I've a little time yet'. Meanwhile, for the Arts Centre Group he bought Battailles, a nine-bedroomed house in Great Dunmow, Essex, with high-ceilinged rooms and nine acres of ornamental gardens. The Revd Jack Philby and wife Pauleen were put in charge. The *Sun* said: 'Cliff buys peace pad for his pals.' The idea was to provide somewhere pleasant and relaxing where Christian media people could meet and share their common concerns and faith.

On Monday, 30 August, BBC TV showed the film *Getaway* which featured Cliff. Filming had taken place in England and in France when he was there in July. There was little dialogue from Cliff in the film, a mere dozen words.

Cliff was at the European Congress on Evangelism in Amsterdam from 28 August to 4 September and, also in September, he appeared on BBC TV's *Nationwide*. On 17 November he appeared on ITV's *Lift Off*, and the

next evening it was the turn of *Top of the Pops*. He appeared on Hospital Radio on 15 December for the Hertfordshire and Essex Hospital in Bishop Stortford.

Press comment on Cliff during 1971 included the following from Lynda Lee Potter in the *Daily Mail*: 'Yesterday in his brown velvet trousers, tight high-necked brown jersey and heavy gold cross he looked like a fervent, fanatical, male Joan of Arc', while Keith Altham in *Record Mirror* said: 'If this really is the age of the anti-hero then Harry Webb may well be fighting a losing battle to be taken seriously, for he is almost infuriatingly nice at a time when being a little nasty goes a long way to providing a strange sort of sincerity.'

Cliff himself said: 'If I fell in love with a girl who wasn't a Christian all I know is that I'd postpone marrying her till I couldn't bear it any more.' Much better, though, was this comment: 'I'd like to marry a girl now who was a combination of Una Stubbs, Cilla Black and Olivia Newton-John.'

1971

Far left: Best joke he's heard for ages

Left: Which do I choose? They both seem rather keen! At the Palladium with the dancers

Cliff's single 'Sing a Song of Freedom', released at the end of 1971, was banned in South Africa, government officials claiming that the lyrics and title 'were slightly permissive'. Mozambique's Laurenco Marques Radio followed suit, since their output was beamed toward South Africa.

Less controversial was Cliff's opening onslaught of 1972 – another thirteen-week BBC 1 TV series of *It's Cliff Richard* beginning on 1 January. For a while Dandy Nichols replaced Una Stubbs, but after Una's son Christian was born the popular lady returned for most of the series. Hank was not in residence this time, but Olivia Newton-John and The Flirtations appeared regularly. The Breakaways supplied the vocal back-up and the Pamela Davis Dancers provided visual delights. Also on Cliff's programme, which featured potential Eurovision songs, were The New Seekers. Elton John popped up as the series progressed. BBC research said the series was two million up in audience ratings compared to the previous year.

While the series was going out on BBC TV Cliff was busy speaking here and there, spending time with the young people of London's Finchley Church, filming in both the House of Commons and House of Lords, and appearing on *Top of the Pops*. In February Cliff made another of his appearances on *Music for Sunday* with music from a variety of people.

On *Top of the Pops* on 2 March he sang his new single 'Jesus', but as with his other religious songs of the time, airplay was limited and sales were not high. It reached a mere thirty-five. The follow-up, 'Living in Harmony', did better and reached number twelve, but the next, 'Brand New Song', gave Cliff his first-ever chart miss. It seems astounding that none of his fans turned out to at least give it a placing! It hardly deserved a total thumbs down.

This was another disappointing singles year for Cliff, which was surprising in view of the extent of his other activities and the popularity of the TV series. Perhaps he was recording the wrong songs. His only album release this year was *The Best of Cliff Volume 2*.

The second week of March saw Cliff singing at a special Tear Fund concert in Manchester. There were two performances. On the children's programme *Ask Aspel* on 12 March, there was an excerpt from a Cliff show in response to a viewer's request. A few days later *Finders Keepers* was shown on television.

Two a Penny came out as a paperback for a throw-away 30p! The *New Musical Express* published a list of the twenty best charting singles over the period 1962-71 and two of Cliff's songs, 'The Young Ones' and 'Bachelor Boy', found themselves in the lower half.

As March progressed Cliff continued to speak of his Christian faith at churches and general gatherings. From the beginning of April until the 8th he was on the Norfolk Broads once more. When he returned he was again caught up in a round of Christian meetings. His Gospel tour from 14 to 27 April prevented his appearance at the *Sun* newspaper awards show in London and instead his award as Top Male Personality (TV) was presented to him in Liverpool where he was appearing on the 14th. It was Cliff's third year of *Sun* success.

Once his British Gospel dates had been fulfilled Cliff flew to Europe on 18 April, returning on the 25th. Cindy Kent went along with Cliff on the British and European dates without her group The Settlers. Not unexpectedly there were rumours that there was a more than friendly relationship between the two. Certainly the lady was stunning.

Cliff's return to Britain saw him involved in some recording sessions for EMI, but again his Christian activities predominated and he attended several conferences at the house he had bought for the Arts Centre Group. His Whit weekend at Battailles saw him in company with a number of Christian artistes. On 29 May he spoke at Norwich Cathedral and the same evening his film *Wonderful Life* was shown on television.

Late in spring the UK Cliff Richard Movement HQ closed down, unable to cope with the thousands of letters that poured in. The ever efficient International Cliff Richard Movement based in Amsterdam took over.

The show-business side of Cliff's career seemed very much to take a back seat at this time. However, plans involving music and variety shows were afoot and on 15 June Cliff was spotted in the company of producer Michael Hurl (who had produced many of Cliff's shows over the years) and Tim Brooke-Taylor. The result of the meeting would become clear on 2 September when Cliff took part in a programme entitled *The Case*.

A twenty-six-concert British tour was announced for 18 October running through to 2 December with some doubles in major cities.

July saw more Christian activities and from 15 to 25 July Cliff was filming for BBC TV in Scandinavia for the television show *The Case*.

On 4 August Cliff appeared on the *Today* programme on Radio Four. He saw a preview of the musical *Jesus Christ Superstar* on the 8th and took in *Godspell* again on the 9th. Two days later he flew to Israel to see for himself the many hallowed Christian and Jewish places. He also gave five concerts in Israel. On 19 August he made an appearance on the BBC 1 *It's Lulu* show. He sang his new single of the time, 'Living in Harmony', plus 'Reason to Believe'. He appeared at the Festival of Jesus in London's Hyde Park on 2 September.

Little did he know that controversy was awaiting him. In September he was due to tour South-East Asia, but as the headline in the British press said: 'Singapore bans long-hair Cliff.' Cliff was hardly a hippy, but his (and The Shadows' later) locks came down over his shirt collar and that was enough – no entry! Apparently the government's aim was to stamp out undesirable elements, but surely not CR? Alas, it was so. Also banned was wearing a wig. South Korea said the same, so Cliff was barred there as well since he didn't feel inclined to cut his hair very short. He carried on with visits to Hong Kong and Japan.

September saw half-a-million copies of a special pop version of St Mark's Gospel (with cartoon drawings) given away as part of a crusade in the north of England. The kit included clues to a pop song based on the Gospel and a reward was offered by Cliff for whoever discovered what it was.

On 6 September the press announced that Cliff would be the British Euro-pop choice for 1973. The music world was stunned by the choice since people thought another face should represent the UK. The singer Malcolm Roberts commented: 'I've waited five years to be involved in Eurovision, but it now looks as if I will have to sing for another country to be given a chance.

'The imagination of the BBC is nil. Cliff is a great artiste but he's done it before. The Continental people have seen Cliff – they want to see a new face.'

Roberts had not been the hot favourite. Olivia Newton-John had. But Bill Cotton, head of the light entertainment section of the BBC, said: 'I was hoping Cliff would star in a BBC series for me next year but his commitments made it impossible. This is a marvellous consolation prize.' Cliff fans purred agreement.

The BBC TV show *The Case* was broadcast in September. It was a comedy and as producer Michael Hurl commented: 'It's the first time Cliff and Tim Brooke-Taylor have worked together – in fact they hadn't met before we started filming – but it worked marvellously. It's like the Bob Hope–Bing Crosby partnership in the "Road" films – it's exactly right.' The script had the two travelling to Scandinavia to make a TV programme. However, they get enmeshed with some bank robbers and there follow car chases, train chases and so on. The *Sun* said the Cliff-Tim partnership was as sound as bacon and eggs, the traditional British breakfast mix.

Tim said: 'I was rather surprised when I was first introduced to Cliff. He's not a rip-roaring tearaway of course. But he's a lot more gutsy in person than the image that seems to come across in some of his shows.'

In early autumn there were more Christian gatherings, yet another visit to *Godspell* (perhaps he was contemplating the part of Jesus?) and of course memories of the fantastic reception he had received in Japan. Many Japanese fans were, from their reports, bowled over, particularly by his rendition of 'My Way'. His final concert on 24 September was followed by a dinner party at the Tokyo Hilton. Cliff and Pat Farrar backed Olivia Newton-John for her singing of 'Just a Little Too Much'. In Indonesia, his first visit, 10,000 wildly appreciative fans saw him at Istora Senayan in Djakarta.

On 14 October Cliff celebrated his thirty-second birthday and Radio Luxembourg played a Cliff record every half-hour. His fan club gave him what he'd asked for – a cassette tape recorder and some blank tapes.

The British tour began in Oxford on 18 October, with Peterborough the last date on 2 December. The Bones and Olivia (wearing a Japanese wedding gown Cliff gave her) supported.

In November Cliff featured 'Brand New Song', which never made the charts, on *Top of the Pops*.

December saw Cliff involved in selecting songs for the British heats of the Eurovision Song Contest and on the 6th he was at the Royal Albert Hall busily raising money for the Arts Centre Group. Gordon Giltrap, Cindy and The Settlers, and Roy Castle were on the bill, plus The Bones and the Brian Bennett Sound. Cliff chose 'I Can't Let You Go' for his opener and sang out with 'Sing a Song of Freedom'. On 11 December Cliff began a two-week spell at the Batley Variety Club once more and at the end of the year he was involved with recording sessions relating to the Eurovision contest.

Away from the immediate headlines was the saga – a long one – of Cliff's back trouble. He explained during the year how one of the vertebrae at the base of his spine hadn't hardened: 'It's much more jellied than it should be . . . I have to lie on the floor and lift first one leg and then the other; then I lift both of them and my back as well, so that I'm arched like a see-saw. There are other exercises too. They only take about five to ten minutes a day but sometimes I forget to do them and get out of the habit. Then I have to begin again as soon as it starts to get painful.'

So 1972 was over. It was a year without major record success. Hopefully 1973 would change that situation.

No wonder some people linked the two romantically! Olivia was on Cliff's 1972 TV series

Following pages: Early shot of Cliff and Shadows boarding an Air France flight to Paris

1972

Cliff singing 'Power to All Our Friends' in the Eurovision Song Contest

Events scheduled for 1973 included a new film, *Take Me High*, a huge Christian festival called Spree, Eurovision and major tours. But what Cliff wanted from the year was simple. He said: 'What I really want is a big hit record. I haven't had one for quite a few years, although people seem to think I have because for some reason I always get a lot of airplay. It's funny really, when I begin to sing some of my more recent songs people clap and move along with the song and I think – if you like it that much, why didn't you go out and buy it?'

Cliff was still preoccupied with his first big single flop, 'Brand New Song'. 'I really couldn't understand it. I played it to my mother and she was sure it'd be a hit.' But it wasn't, and this was strange. Eurovision gave him singles blues relief.

Out of a total of 250 songs, six were selected for the final list of possible songs for the British 1973 entry which Cliff would sing. They were previewed by Cliff in the Cilla Black series on BBC TV. All six featured on her 24 February show and the winner was to be announced the following week, 3 March.

The six contenders were 'Come Back Billy Joe' from famed songwriters Mitch Murray and Tony Macaulay; 'Ashes to Ashes' from Tony Cole; 'Tomorrow Rising' by Brian Bennett and Mike Hawker; 'Help It Along' from Christopher Neil; 'Power to All Our Friends' by Guy Fletcher and Doug Flett; and 'The Days of Love' by Alan Hawkshaw and Douggie Wright. 'Power to All Our Friends' was chosen, a rousing hymn-anthem which set British hopes high for the contest.

The record of 'Power to All Our Friends' came out with 'Come Back Billie Joe' on the flip side. It was Cliff's biggest hit since his last Eurovision smash of 1968, the chart-topping 'Congratulations'. 'Power to All Our Friends' didn't get quite as high but it made number five.

The final was held in Luxembourg on 7 April and it turned out rather a sad affair really. Cliff scored 123 points and ahead was Spain with 125 and the host country Luxembourg with 129. Just before the contest Cliff undertook some minor surgery – not to himself, but to the lyrics of the song. For months Cliff had sung

'Laying in the sun at Monte Carlo'
but correct grammar ruled the day
and the line was changed to 'Lying in
the sun'. The BBC light
entertainment boss Billy Cotton said:
'Cliff's grammar ought to be got
right.'

Cliff was very disappointed by his
score in the contest and in a rather
depressed moment he told the press;
'I think I'm now too old ever to win. I
feel it would be unwise for
professional reasons to appear again
in a contest like this for at least five
years. Then I'd be thirty-eight, a bit
of an old-age pensioner for song
contests I think.' Certainly the BBC
had pulled out all stops to make
people aware of the song. The
Executive Producer of Radio Two,
Geoffrey Owen, called on programme
organizers in the German, French,
Italian, Portuguese and Yugoslavian
sections to familiarize their listeners
with the British song. The story
appeared in the *Sunday Times* on 1
April 1973.

Success may not have come in the
supreme accolade of being placed
first, but as with 'Congratulations',
the record proved a universal
favourite. It topped the charts in
Holland, Israel, Sweden and
Luxembourg and reached number
three in a Hong Kong radio hit
parade listing.

Inevitably newspapers conducted a
post mortem on the event and various
commentators questioned the whole
contest and the type of song which
was featured. This question even
exercised some writers before the
contest. James Thomas in the *Daily
Express* said the six selected favourites
offered a display of musical
mediocrity. He said the whole thing
represented a misunderstanding of
popular taste. Be that as it may,
'Power to All Our Friends' gave Cliff
his biggest hit for five years.

No Cliff year rests on one event and
1973 was no exception – there was
much else in store for him.

The other really big event of 1973
was the film *Take Me High*, originally
called *Hot Property*. Cliff worked on the
film from early June to the first week
of August. Three weeks of shooting
took place in the Birmingham area
and the rest at Elstree. At the same
time that he began filming for *Take Me
High* there was a premiere in London
of *Why Should the Devil Have All the Good*

Music, which listed Cliff and Larry Norman in the main credits. It presented the comings and goings of the 1972 London Festival for Jesus with premiere evenings from 5 to 7 June.

Take Me High had its premiere at the ABC, Shaftesbury Avenue, London, on Friday, 14 December, with a charity gala at Birmingham on the 20th. Cliff at this time was in cabaret at Sheffield's Fiesta. It went on general release on Boxing Day, 26 December, mainly in the London area. The title track of the new movie was issued as a single with the album soundtrack expected early in 1974.

Cliff's leading lady in the film was Debbie Watling, twenty-five years old. She was the daughter of actor Jack Watling. In the film, his first in seven years, Cliff sang twelve songs. He played a rich young city gent called Tim Matthews who is dispatched to the Midland city of Birmingham to establish a major

hamburger restaurant and in consequence destroys a rival concern. During his exploits he falls in love with Sarah, played by Debbie Watling. In Thailand the film was entitled *The Heavenly Sounds*!

In the concert field, Cliff had spent the early part of the year in cabaret at London's famed Talk of the Town. He began on 22 February with the show commencing at 11 pm. The previous day there had been a photo-call.

On 25 February Cliff sang at St Paul's Cathedral as part of an eight-week series of concerts presented there by the Revd Jack Philby.

On 13 April he was headed for Australia, arriving at Perth on the 14th at 14.20 on flight AL 308. It was part of his Gospel ministry and he was accompanied by Bill Latham and the Revd David MacInnes, the Precentor of Birmingham Cathedral. Wherever he went there was a 'full house' sign. Cliff sang songs which expressed

man's search for meaning and epitomized his cry for help. Cliff sang other songs of hope. He visited Australia again in October and at the Sydney Opera House he was joined by comedian Harry Secombe.

In Britain Spree was a major religious event in late summer, running from 27 August to 1 September. Spree stood for Spiritual Re-Emphasis. Cliff appeared on 31 August and at the special final occasion at Wembley on 1 September.

The autumn saw a mixture of pop and Gospel concerts in Britain with the latter centred on six provincial cities. During all this hectic activity in Britain, Cliff found time to fly to Essen on 29 September where he received the Silver Lion from the German branch of Radio Luxembourg.

Another major event of the autumn took place on 17 September when Cliff presented a charity show called

An *Evening With Cliff Richard* in aid of the John Groom Homes. It was a new act and one which obviously had future tour dates in mind. There was the usual and very popular medley of hits, material from the forthcoming *Take Me High*, some religious songs and a new rock and roll medley at the end. The final songs were 'I Could Easily Fall', 'Higher Ground' and 'Visions'. After the inevitable stamping for more he came back and sang 'Power to All Our Friends'. He left the stage with the band playing 'Sing a Song of Freedom'.

At the end of the year he appeared on *Sunday Night at the London Palladium* and then had some rest.

Another year was over. There were many things to reflect on, not least his continued ability to handle two diaries, secular and religious.

He commented to me in 1973: 'I've always enjoyed hard work. And I like my work. Everything is well planned for me!' This is a side of a star's life which often goes unnoticed – the devoted people behind the scenes rarely receive the praise they are due.

Cliff also revealed during the year how his dog Kelly came into his life. 'A make-up girl at the BBC bought him for £3 and told me he was a pedigree Labrador. I said, "What? a pedigree Labrador for £3 – don't you believe it." But she did.

'However, she already had an Afghan hound, and when she took Kelly home the two dogs didn't get on together. Then another girl said she'd take him, but her husband didn't like keeping dogs. So I said I'd take him. Of course, he wasn't a pedigree – he was an all-sorts. Like all mongrels, he's much more affectionate than most dogs seem to be.'

Less wholesome was Cliff's story about how when he was younger in India he tried to eat lizards. 'I've been told my Dad often used to dive across the floor just in time to stop me popping a lizard in my mouth, because there were lizards everywhere!'

Opposite: Dilys Watling joins with Cliff for a song from *Take Me High*

Below: Precious Kelly, his dog

Bottom: Cliff and The Three Degrees, British hit-makers from 1974 onwards, later heroes of Prince Charles

'I don't think show business is full of wicked people – there are good and bad just like in any other field.

'Out of the sixty-three records I've made, sixty-two have got into the top thirty. So I don't think I need to do anything spectacular like David Bowie to stay successful.

'I haven't asked Olivia to marry me.'

So spoke Cliff in 1974. The oft-maligned artiste was keeping himself busy – fresh as ever – in his sixteenth show-business year. Appropriately enough, 1974 saw the issue of a handsomely packaged eighty-five-track set of Cliff albums (seven tracks were from The Shadows) at £9.85 from World Records. Six albums, colour album-sleeve pictures, and booklet made up the package. Its tracking from 'Move It' to 'Take Me High' gave an arresting insight into the man who roared back into the top ten during 1974 just when record dealers, if not fans, were wondering whether he would have another blockbuster to keep up his momentum and (for dealers) the sales tills ringing.

Cliff's UK record output consisted of fifty-seven singles up to December 1973, forty-four EPs and twenty-nine albums. Of the singles, nineteen had been silver discs (sales of 250,000), and three were British golds (one million sales). The three were Living Doll/Apron Strings, The Young Ones/We Say Yeah and The Next Time/Bachelor Boy. The best disc run had been between July 1959 when Living Doll/Apron Strings was issued and November 1963 when Don't Talk To Him/Say You're Mine appeared. During this period eighteen of his discs struck silver or gold.

In 1974, interviewed by this writer for television, Cliff summed up his career up to this point as one in which he had made the music he liked and had given much pleasure and entertainment to thousands across the world. He reacted strongly against the view that he had lost his own generation and made no impression upon the next. He believed his material had become socially aware, that it was not a succession of love songs.

One event of 1974 reminded Cliff of a dimension to life other than just providing pleasure. On Tear Fund Sunday, 3 March, a new twenty-

minute film strip, narrated by Cliff, gave his impressions of a visit he had made to Bangladesh towards the end of 1973. Pictures were by Clifford Shirley who had been with Cliff, along with George Hoffman and Bill Latham. In his book, *Which One's Cliff*, Cliff gives further comments on the profound impression which this visit had upon him.

Another event of the year gave fans a tremendous thrill. This was the International Cliff Richard Movement's first ever fan club get-together which took place at Hornsey Town Hall, The Broadway, London N8, on Tuesday, 9 July, from 3.30 to 7.00 pm. A limited attendance of 800 was imposed by the organizers, with correspondence being dealt with by Annette Bauer who had worked tirelessly for fans over the past few years. The event included a visit from Cliff, a chance to ask him some questions, the film strip of Cliff in Bangladesh and a screening of the film *A Day in the Life of Cliff Richard* made by Dutch TV in the early 1970s.

Among the things Cliff talked about were his new newly recorded album *The 31st of February Street*, his favourite film (*Summer Holiday*) and Bangladesh. He accompanied himself on guitar and sang 'Congratulations', 'Power to All Our Friends', 'Fireside Song' and 'Help It Along'. His final song was 'Living Doll'. Cliff's friend Bill Latham talked about Tear Fund. Cliff stayed and watched the Tear Fund film strip, *Love Never Gives Up*, and afterwards announced the winner of the Tear Fund raffle which had books and records of his as prizes. Tear Fund was fairly prominent in Cliff's life during the year.

Many at the fan club event in Hornsey had been at Southall Football Ground in the first week of January when staff of *Buzz* (a teenage religious magazine) and the Swedish Gospel singers Choralerna had met each other in a football match. Cliff appeared in the football match, his first for twenty years, and was sent off for fouling a player, although the circumstances seemed most suspicious. He had come on for the Buzz All Stars during the second half and had played for ten minutes only. The referee Basil Smith took the unusual action of sending Cliff off and then summoning him back on to get

him to sign his name in the referee's book! Referee Smith was heard to say: 'It was the only way I could get his autograph.' More than 1,000 people watched the match, with both teams agreeing that the crowd had come to see Cliff and not their own dubious football skills, save for the Buzz captain John Kilford, a former Leeds United player who was studying at Oak Hill Theological College.

Cliff gave a series of Scottish concerts for Tear Fund late in October, while profits from his album *Help It Along*, comprising specifically religious material, were also donated to Tear Fund. During the year Cliff was presented with a £12,000 cheque for Tear Fund. The money was spent on buying an ambulance for a Zambian hospital, a Land Rover with medical equipment for India, a new X-ray machine for Nigeria, and a rehabilitation programme for Bangladesh.

Cliff was also busy during 1974 raising money for the Arts Centre Group and it was announced during

Perhaps I should use both eyes

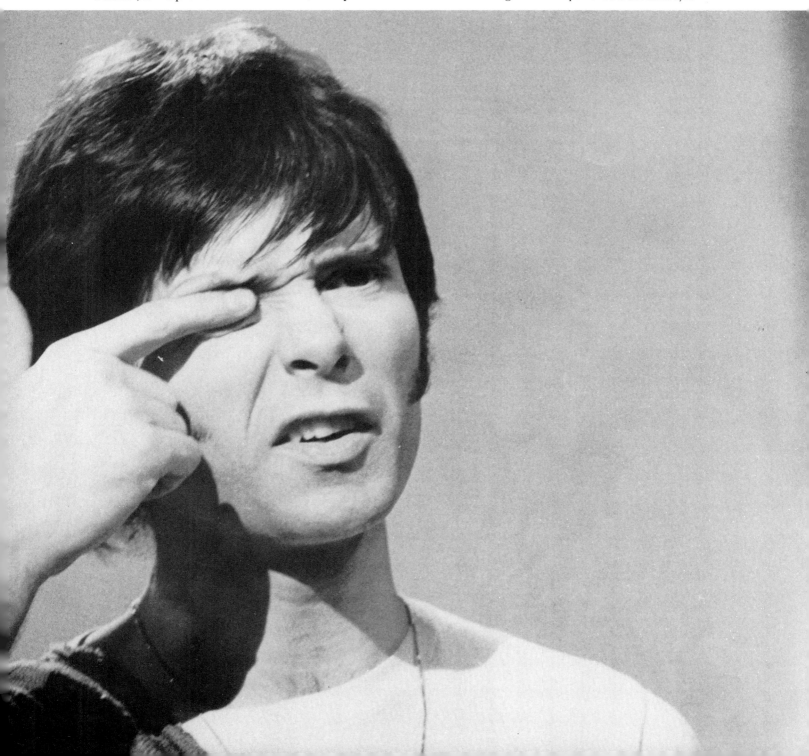

the year that he would give concerts in Manchester, Newcastle, Sheffield and Leicester at the beginning of 1975. Another concert in the New Year would be 'In the Name of Jesus' where Cliff, Choralerna and guests Malcolm and Alwyn would sing. The proceeds would go to Tear Fund and Musical Gospel Outreach.

Apart from his charitable and fan club activities Cliff was busy with television and touring. His own BBC TV series, *It's Cliff Richard*, was later in the year, in August. He made a number of guest appearances on other people's BBC shows. In May he was on *Look – Mike Yarwood*. Mike asked him who he had brought along to sing on the programme.

Cliff replied: 'Well, actually, I've brought along me.'

Mike: 'Good for you, good for you. And what are you going to do for us tonight?'

Cliff: 'I'm going to sing my latest recording.'

It was 'You Keep Me Hangin' On'.

The same month he was on the *Nana Mouskouri Show*. He sang 'Give Me Back That Old Familiar Feeling', 'Constantly' and 'I Believe in Music'. He appeared as a puppet in *Play It Again, Stewpot* (the puppet sang 'You Keep Me Hangin' On').

The first of his 1974 series of television programmes for the BBC was on 24 August. He sported a black and white checked jacket and black trousers. Among his songs were 'Give Me Back That Old Familiar Feeling', 'You Keep Me Hangin' On', 'I'll Love You to Want Me', 'Summer Holiday' and 'Bachelor Boy'. The Nolan Sisters and Hank were among the guests. It was a six-week series. The final show was on 28 September with Cliff doing a tap-dance routine at the beginning of the programme. Among his songs on this last programme of the series was 'A Matter of Moments', 'Why Me Lord', 'I'm Leaving It All Up to You' (during which he impersonated Donny Osmond), 'Pigeon', 'Rolling on the River' and, as a finale, 'Visions'.

During the year he took part in various religious programmes, including Radio Two's *Pause for Thought*. He also appeared on foreign radio and television, on the popular Dutch show compered by Eddy Brecker, and in Australia where Sydney TV twice showed *Help, Hope and Hallelujah*, the film of a Cliff Gospel concert.

There were a few disappointments. One involved a BBC TV spectacular which was due to be filmed in Hong Kong. Six months of painstaking preparation suffered a deadly blow when Cliff succumbed to back trouble. He was ill on another occasion during 1974 when he had bronchitis, laryngitis and pharyngitis, which meant he missed three nights at the London Palladium. Rolf Harris had the unenviable task of standing in. Most disappointed possibly was a party from Holland, but when Cliff was next in the country he invited the group to his hotel.

Cliff played the Palladium in London along with a number of other artistes from 3 April to 11 May. He said 'it was great to be back' and recalled his last appearance at the famous theatre. This had taken place during the fuel crisis and the lights went out just as he was going to sing 'Power to All Our Friends', which was part of his usual Palladium programme. He also sang familiars like 'In the Country', 'Next Time', 'Dancing Shoes', 'Constantly', 'On the Beach' and 'Give Me Back That Old Familiar Feeling'. There were a number of film clips and then more songs, including 'Amazing Grace' and 'Living in Harmony'. He previewed his forthcoming single 'You Keep Me Hanging On'. At the end he sang 'Congratulations', 'Power to All Our Friends' and, as was his custom at this time, 'Visions' for his finale.

Together with The Shadows he gave a special concert at the Palladium in October in aid of the dependants of Colin Charman who was one of the producers of *Top of the Pops* and sadly had died.

His British tour, which had some extra Gospel dates pencilled in just before it began, ran from Thursday, 7 November, to 14 December, opening at the Odeon, Birmingham, and climaxing at Hull City Hall. Two Gospel concerts which preceded the pop tour were at Port Talbot where 5,000 heard him at the Afan Lido. A second concert was arranged at the last minute to meet overwhelming demand for tickets. The general tour covered eighteen cities and took in twenty-three concerts, including four

evenings at the Double Diamond, Caerphilly.

This was the year in which Cliff went back to his school, now renamed Rivermead School, where he joined their Dramatic Society to play Bottom in Shakespeare's *Midsummer Night's Dream*. The play opened on 3 July and, with a break on the 9th and 10th, closed on 12 July. Cliff had begun rehearsing on 9 June.

In the recording field, 1974 saw the continuing success of 'Take Me High', issued in December 1973, which reached twenty-seven. The follow-up, 'You Keep Me Hangin' On', fared well in reaching thirteen but there was indecision in the Cliff camp about what else to record and release. The next year was to show this quite clearly and rather disastrously. Cliff's 1974 album releases were the religious *Help It Along* and the rather underrated *The 31st of February Street* which did show signs that Cliff's recording career might possibly be on the mend. All of us hoped this would be so.

Giving all at a big night at the Palladium – The Shadows come together once more and appear with Cliff for charity

Above: 1975 Bratislava Song Festival

Opposite: Saying hello to friends and neighbours at London's Talk of the Town

It was Britain forever! Cliff told the nation: 'I couldn't care if they taxed me ninety per cent of my earnings – I would scrape by. I like it here. I've been all over the world and there's no place like it.'

Home-loving he certainly was, yet, as every fan knows, he travelled the world each and every year. One new country promised unusual delights for Cliff in 1975 – Russia! He was very much in line to become the first UK artiste to record in the Soviet Union. A 'draft' agreement was announced which would take Cliff to Russia to record an album of Russian songs.

EMI spokesman Paul Braithwaite said: 'We seem to have reached the stage where pop music is now acceptable in Russia and they are prepared to record Western artistes.'

Why Cliff? Braithwaite said EMI Britain received more requests for Cliff from Russians than for any other of their recording artistes. 'He seems to have quite a following there despite the fact that his records have never been exported to the USSR. The Russians do, however, listen a lot to Western radio.'

Elsewhere in the world Cliff was still very much to the fore. Korean MBC TV showed *Cliff in Korea* on 3 January (it had been recorded in 1969), a two-record 'live' album set of Cliff was issued in Japan, he visited Portugal as part of his Tear Fund

interests, and during March and April he toured Europe, the emphasis being on television shows and recordings. In Denmark he recorded a special *Cliff in Copenhagen*; in Germany there was *Hits a Gogo*; in Holland it was *The National Hit Parade*; Austria meant *Spotlight*; and in France he appeared on *Bouvard en liberté*.

Hong Kong issued *Cliff Richard's Greatest Hits Volume 2*. Belgium released *The Best of Cliff Richard*, and in Australia *Cliff Entertains (Cliff Richard at the Opera House)* appeared.

Later in the year, on 29 and 30 September, he again appeared on Dutch TV and it was Holland which in October saw one of Cliff's few promotional efforts for his single 'Honky-Tonk Angel'. This was the record which caused one of the few 'scandals' to have afflicted Cliff during his career.

His first single of the year, 'It's Only Me You've Left Behind', released in March, had failed to chart, and a major hit was once more badly needed. 'Honky-Tonk Angel' seemed to be one of Cliff's strongest discs for some time – it was the lyrics which caused the trouble. A honky-tonk is US slang for a sordid nightclub, and a honky-tonk angel means a prostitute. According to one report, Cliff learnt the meaning of the song during a religious meeting at the major evangelical Christian centre at

Hildenborough Hall, Kent, where he was speaking, which couldn't have been more embarrassing. Cliff apparently thought the song was simply, as he put it, 'a tribute to love and the goodness of women'. As soon as he realized what the words meant he said he hoped his record would be a flop and played no further part in its promotion.

There was some airplay for the record but fans took heed of what Cliff said and showed no real disposition to buy 'Honky-Tonk Angel'. It was a hit in several countries but in Britain it was another chart miss. Any misery which might have come to Cliff and fans from this affair was compounded by the fact that 1975 was one of the most disastrous record times ever for Cliff. Both his singles failed to chart. And there was no album release. Oddly though, and not for the first time in these circumstances, Cliff was extremely busy in general media circles and he certainly wasn't hidden from the public. The year saw Cliff constantly on television. There was a major British pop Gospel tour lasting for several months late in the year, and he made frequent appearances at major religious gatherings. The only explanation for his poor record success probably lies in a lack of positive musical direction and/or a dearth of good song material for an artiste of his style.

Cliff's 1975 television programme schedule included *Top of the Pops* on 20 March for the single 'It's Only Me You've Left Behind'. Tony Blackburn was the compere. He said Cliff's disc would be his radio 'Record of the Week' and he thought it was 'fabulous'. Cliff was attired in a smart grey suit for *Top of the Pops* and during his performance he danced to the music rather than merely clapping to the beat.

The popular *Saturday Scene* on ITV on 19 April provided Cliff with another valuable promotional outlet. His old number 'Travellin' Light' was played and when he and Sally James, the compere, began their conversation Cliff pointed out there was a newer and better version of the song on his album *The 31st of February Street*. He told Sally he thought the album was one of his best in every way, even down to the sleeve and the album title. Sally remarked on the fact that there were five song credits to Cliff.

Honest Cliff said it was really only four and a half, pointing out that the title track was just one minute long.

Cliff was a special guest on the popular *Jim'll Fix It* show. Helen Moon of Cromer had written to the programme saying what she would love more than anything would be a meeting with Cliff. And when the meeting came, Helen thought Cliff was much more beautiful in the flesh than he appears on television or on stage. Apart from spending time with Cliff and Jimmy, Helen received a signed copy of *31st of February*. Cliff also appeared on *This Is Your Life* when the subject was Richard O'Sullivan. The actor had appeared in the Cliff films *The Young Ones* and *Wonderful Life*.

From 24 February to 2 March southern Britain saw Cliff contribute a week of late-night religious epilogues in the *Guidline* TV series. On the BBC 2 TV *In Concert* series in the summer Cliff sang his new version of 'Travellin' Light', 'The Singer', 'No Matter What', 'The Leaving' and 'You Will Never Know'. His closing items were 'Yesterday, Today, Forever', then 'Love On' (a new song) and 'Nothing to Remind Me'. He wore his by now familiar denim gear.

On 6 and 13 September Cliff starred in two shows called *It's Cliff and Friends*. The first show had guests Alan Shiers, David Copperfield and Su Shiffron. Cliff wore a red T-shirt and blue jeans and opened the show with 'All You Need Is Love'. Other numbers were 'Good on the Sally Army' (the flip side of 'Yes He Lives!' in 1978), and 'I've Got Time'. He sang a duet with Su entitled 'For You'. In programme two Cliff featured 'Love Train', 'Move It', 'Ob La Di, Ob La Da', 'Up in Canada' and the song which was to cause trouble, 'Honky-Tonk Angel'. He sang a duet with Australian artiste Debbie Burns and introduced as a special guest Simon Townshend, brother of the famous Pete of The Who.

The same month saw a blue-denim-suited Cliff sing 'Honky-Tonk Angel' on the pop TV show *Supersonic*, a week before he began to question the song's lyrics. He also sang 'Let's Have a Party' and did a brief but much appreciated impression of Elvis. A third *It's Cliff and Friends* made the

Above: Hey, this is fun – frolics on a TV set

Opposite: In between shots during a 1974 TV programme – quite obviously things are going well

TV screens before the end of 1975 on 27 December. Cliff sang 'All I've Got Is Music', 'Miss You Nights' (his next single and the record which saw him back in the charts), 'Gee Whizz It's You', 'A Star in the Sky' (with a school choir), 'Ding Dong Merrily on High', 'Hark the Herald Angels Sing', 'Once in Royal David's City' and 'O Come All Ye Faithful'.

Cliff was also busy during the year with radio shows. He had a thirteen-week series from Easter Sunday to 22 June for Radio One and Two on the religious morning spot on Sundays, *Gospel Road*, replacing Alistair Pirie. The format was a mix of Cliff singing, interviewing and playing music, live and on record, by a variety of Christian musicians. A further *Gospel Road* series was announced for the early part of 1976.

Cliff's records found their way into numerous shows. He did some session work with Paul Williams producing recordings for BBC programmes, and

there was a recording for Capital Radio's *Xmas Day Special*.

Cliff's live concert work began early in the New Year on a Gospel footing. He was rehearsing on 1 January for a week's tour of the UK from 18 to 22 January with Swedish gospel choir Choralerna. The special events involving both were two concerts, 'In the Name of Jesus', at London's Royal Albert Hall on 18 and 25 January. Many thought the evenings ended on a marvellous note with the singing of 'Amazing Grace'.

On 19 April Cliff was at the Empire Pool, Wembley, for a 'Way to Life' rally. He sat and talked on stage with friend Bill Latham and the occasion's main evangelist Dick Saunders. Some of Cliff's speech, along with other highlights from the concerts, was broadcast in a short feature on the Radio Four religious magazine programme *Sunday*.

His autumn Gospel concert tour ran from 9 to 25 October. He was supported on his first six tour dates by Water Into Wine, a Gospel group based in Cambridge. Cliff's songs on the tour included 'Day by Day', 'Mr Business Man', 'Joy of Living', 'Everything Is Beautiful', 'Love Song' (Cliff referred to Olivia Newton-John having recorded the song), 'Help It Along', 'Up in Canada', 'Love Never Gives Up', 'Higher Ground', 'When I Survey the Wondrous Cross' and 'We Shall Be Changed'.

His secular tour followed immediately upon the Gospel dates, beginning on 30 October at the Odeon, Hammersmith, London, and finishing at Sunderland's Empire Theatre on 22 November.

Cliff's tour repertoire included (as sung at Hammersmith) 'The Singer', 'Living in Harmony', 'Living Doll', 'Gee Whizz It's You', 'Good on the Sally Army', 'Move It', 'The Minute You're Gone', 'Up in Canada', 'Why Should the Devil Have All the Good Music', 'All My Love', 'Love On', 'Back Home', 'All I Have to Do Is Dream', 'Who Love's You Pretty Baby', 'You Make Me Feel Brand New', 'Listen to the Music', and 'Miss You Nights'.

There was cabaret during 1975 at The Talk of the Town, where Cliff's programme was somewhat different from that of his tour. He included 'Rock and Roll (I Gave You the Best Years of My Life)', 'I Can't Let You Go', 'When a Man Loves a Woman', 'When I'm Sixty-four', 'I Wish We'd All Been Ready', 'When I Survey the Wondrous Cross', 'Let's Have a Party', 'Johnny Be Good', 'Help It Along'. With Bruce Welch he sang 'Bachelor Boy' and 'Living Doll', and then continued with 'Let Me Be the One', the Eurovision Shadows entry of 1975, 'Power to All Our Friends', 'The Love I Lost', 'If You Don't Know Me By Now' and 'Love Train'. Cliff began rehearsing for The Talk of the Town on 18 June. Opening night was 20 June and the run ended on 5 July.

There was a surfeit of other events, including the *Sun* awards and a dinner at London's Hilton Hotel, a Variety Club Luncheon in honour of Vera Lynn, a charity concert in Manchester for the appeal sponsored by Piccadilly Radio, Manchester, for the families of Sgt Williams and P.C. Rodgers, two policeman who had died from injuries received during rioting in the city. There was *Look Alive* for ITV, a nostalgia show for Capital Radio, London, with Roger Scott the DJ recalling 1959, and Hospital Radio interviews. He went back to his old school for a dinner and to EMI studios for more recordings.

It was a busy year, not without controversy, not without record disappointments, yet full of media and other engagements. He was as popular as ever.

1975

It was like old times. Cliff was back in the singles charts with a vengeance. 'Miss You Nights' came into the charts in February and reached number fifteen. The follow-up, 'Devil Woman', made the top ten, first appearing in the charts during May. The hat-trick came with 'I Can't Ask for Anything More Than You Babe'. It settled for position seventeen with a first entry in August. A fourth hit came with 'Hey Mr Dream Maker', though in comparison with the others its final chart position of thirty-one was rather disappointing. And it gave warning that perhaps Cliff's singles comeback was not yet quite firing on all cylinders. But 1976 was a good chart year.

The year also saw Cliff's first album since 1974 and it certainly was a good one. It had a tongue-in-cheek title – *I'm Nearly Famous*.

Cliff's success with 'Miss You Nights' was not confined to Britain. It provided him at long last with a potential breakthrough into the US market. Its success across the Atlantic led to a postponement of his trip to Russia. His immediate reaction to the single's success was predictable – he was really excited in a manner he had not been for years. Elton John raved over the disc and it was he who said his company Rocket must release it in the States, where it was issued early in the year. The Americans sent it into their charts. It began an era in which Cliff showed he could hit the US Hot 100, with some interruptions maybe, but overall proving that he could become a considerable success with US record buyers.

Cliff made his trip to Russia in August and it opened the way for the release in 1979 of the material which he had recorded in the Soviet Union. EMI and the Soviet Department of Trade signed contracts late in 1976 for the release of *The Best of Cliff Richard Volume 1* and his latest album *I'm Nearly Famous*, though one wonders what Russian fans must have made of the title!

Cliff's musicians for Russia were Brian Bennett, Terry Britten, Kevin Peek, Cliff Hall, Graham Jarvis, Dave Richmond, Tony Rivers and John Perry. There were twelve concerts in Leningrad and eight in Moscow, with two matinées in each city.

Cliff had a rapturous reception which led him to say 'rock 'n' roll is

the international language', and if he was not allowed to transport his earnings to the West at least it seemed a major breakthrough in terms of his career and prestige. As his agent, the long-standing and enthusiastic Eddie Jarrett, said: 'You don't go to Russia for money anyway.' Eddie had set the ball rolling as far back as 1974.

Cliff also visited the United States. 'Until now I had always said I am not going there until something happens – I'm not saying I'm me and having nothing to talk about.' He covered nine cities and somehow made it from East Coast to West, some 3,000 miles with considerable variations of musical taste along the way. He promised the Americans he would be back for a summer tour in 1977.

Russia and America were not the only countries which gave him an enthusiastic welcome. In the early part of April he had concerts in Denmark and Sweden and June was spent in Japan. Dutch fans were thrilled by a visit to Holland for the purpose of recording a fifty-minute TV special on their famed *Eddy Go Round Show*.

When news of his Japanese visit was announced there was an immediate cry from Hong Kong Cliff fans for a visit there en route. This he did from 14 to 19 June, holding a press conference on the 16th and giving three well received concerts. A meeting for fans was organized at the Lee Gardens Hotel on his last day. He answered questions, some Chinese musicians played, and Cliff plus acoustic guitar serenaded the fans with music from *Summer Holiday*.

Cliff's French album *Cliff chante en français* was at long last issued in mid-February. British fans were not neglected. There was a Gospel tour from 2 to 16 October and on the first of the month he was at Ireland's RDS Concert Hall in Dublin. His secular tour opened at the Odeon, Birmingham, on 22 October and closed at the Glasgow Apollo on the 27th.

The year had opened with Cliff's TV series, *It's Cliff and Friends*, carrying over from 1975. The second programme was transmitted on 3 January and the series came to an end with the eighth show on 14 February, Valentine's Day. On his first show of the year guests included Richard Kerr and Adge Webber and the group

1976

Opposite: Are you watching carefully? *Cinderella*, London Palladium December 1976

1976

Reaction. Swiss artiste Olivia Gray was a guest on the third show of the series, as also were The Jesters and London singer Sam Leano. Angie Miller, Mike Onions (said to have been a Mr Universe), Cotton Lloyd and Christians were on show four, and for the fifth it was Tony Adams, Alexander John – a talented singer-songwriter from Yugoslavia – and a girl rock group called Superior, formerly called Mother Superior. It comprised Lesley Sly, Jackie Crew, Audrey Swinburne and Jackie Badger. Their new single was 'Love the One You're With'. The name change came because of 'what Cliff stands for and his involvement with Christianity – we thought it might be better to call the girls just Superior', said producer Phil Bishop. Cliff agreed and further commented: 'I do think Mother Superior is pretty tasteless for a rock group', though he softened the criticism by adding that he thought their record was terrific.

His policy of having new and relatively unknown artistes on this particular series continued in programme six with appearances by David and June Brooks, comedians the Black Abbots and the Surprise Sisters. His show on 7 February included comedian Les Brian and a dance group called Systematic. The final show featured George Moody backed by Skyline, a magic act by Los Magicos, and Shona Lang, a promising New Zealand singer on the EMI label who joined with Cliff in singing 'Jumbalaya'. Cliff, who wore blue trousers and jacket with green stripes round the edges, reminded viewers it was Valentine's Day and said that he had himself posted fifteen cards but only – mysteriously he thought – received fourteen in reply. He produced a huge envelope from the fan club and pulled out the very tiny card inside it! He closed the series by singing 'I'm Nearly Famous' and then 'Visions'. 'Thank you. Goodnight. God Bless,' were his final words.

'Miss You Nights' gave him at long last another slot in *Top of the Pops* on 29 January with Tony Blackburn compering. He sang the hit on *Supersonic* on 14 February, wearing a white jacket and trousers, and a green shirt. He was back on *Top of the Pops* on 26 February sporting his familiar blue denim suit for the rehearsal but a dark green suit, white shirt and green and black tie for the actual filming.

Radio play was extensive during February and March with Radio One DJ Paul Burnette, in particular, praising the record highly.

'Devil Woman', released in May, gained media momentum with *Saturday Scene*, Radio One's *Insight*, Capital Radio's *Hullabaloo*, and Manchester's Piccadilly Radio being amongst the main promotion points as 1976 continued to prove itself a good year for Cliff.

His Christian work continued, with several major events during the year. A new series of *Gospel Road* began on 4 January with long-time friend Cindy Kent reviewing records and Cliff pursuing the established format of himself singing a few songs and otherwise introducing other acts. At Wembley on 24 April there was the annual 'Way to Life' rally with Cliff speaking about Tear Fund at the 4pm meeting and giving his testimony as well as singing a few songs at the evening gathering.

London had its first Meeting House for Cliff fans in May 1976 when Janet Johnson decided there should be one. She had been for a long time, and is still, a major Cliff fan and a tireless worker in fan activities.

Other odds and ends of the year included a special ceremony with World Records staff on 8 June when it was learnt that his six-record box, released in 1974, had made over £350,000. The Managing Director, Derek Sinclair, made the presentation as it was he who had masterminded the whole attractive package. Cliff changed from using Gibson guitars to Martin. One hundred and six tracks were featured in a six-cassette series called *The Music and Life of Cliff Richard*. And it was reported that £25,000 had been raised from the 1975 Tear Fund Gospel concerts.

The year had brought the adrenalin back into Cliff's bloodstream. His records were in vogue again and he was in demand not only in the UK but also in unexpected quarters: the United States and, more surprisingly, Russia.

For once a rather serious Cliff

Opposite: Cliff at the Scripture Union HQ, London, with members of the media team

Right: Members of the Cliff Richard Fan Club of Manchester, whose organizer is Alan Elliott, with Piccadilly Radio DJ Dave Ward and the man himself

Below: A guitar-shaped birthday cake for Cliff from Joan Gallagher and Janet Johnson

1977

Alas, 1977 was not as successful as 1976. The record revival of the previous twelve months was not maintained. The first single of the year, 'My Kinda Life', reached number fifteen, but the follow-up, 'When Two Worlds Drift Apart', made only forty-six. There were no other single releases.

The 1977 album release in the secular market was *Every Face Tells a Story*, which did quite well. The Gospel album was *Small Corners* and it was much appreciated. So at least the long-players made up for another bout of singles flu. And in the autumn there was a special compilation album, *Cliff Richard's 40 Golden Greats*.

The most important event of the year was the publication of his new book, *Which One's Cliff*, in September. In it Cliff told his story to friend Bill Latham. The emphasis was on personal beliefs and attitudes rather than on Cliff's record and show-business life. It was an instant success and established a book-signing record for London's major store in Oxford Street, Selfridges. Cliff signed 333 books an hour, which according to the store's experts in these matters was well above the previous high scores of

Edward Heath, former British Prime Minister (230), and another former Premier, Harold Wilson (225). The book contained few surprises but it answered the basic questions which people ask of Cliff and with which he had wrestled over the years – his faith and show business, his bachelorhood, and so forth.

There was considerable promotion by Cliff for the book. It sold around 100,000 copies in hardback form, in addition to which very high sales were to come in the several paperback editions.

During interviews about the book Cliff added a few other thoughts on his life:

'While I'm an entertainer I've got this marvellous platform for my religion. I'd be undercutting my appeal if I gave it up. Who would come and see the Revd Richard?'

'I do a lot of walking these days as well, that pleases my dog Kelly. If she's lucky I'll take her round the local golf course and that's quite a long way. She really misses me when I'm away and I miss her a lot too. I don't like going for a walk myself that much. There doesn't seem much point to it somehow. Having a dog bounding along makes all the

difference.' Did that mean he was lonely? Many a heart must have fluttered at the thought of helping out.

Early in 1977 rumours began that Cliff and The Shadows would get together for some dates on a tour to be called 'Kicks', or this at least was the thought in the International Cliff Richard Movement magazine *Dynamite*. And still fresh in Cliff's mind was his unannounced visit to India and Bangladesh in December 1976. His thoughts and impressions were given in a Tear Fund film strip sequel to *Love Never Gives Up*. It was called *Loved Into Life* and was issued in April. A further Tear Fund Gospel tour was announced for 1977. The Fund also issued the film *A World of Difference* which looked at the problems of the Third World through the eyes of its director George Hoffman. Cliff made a contribution to the film.

The Tear Fund Gospel tour opened at the Carn Brae Leisure Centre between Redruth and Camborne, Cornwall, on 7 October, the last concert taking place at Ipswich Gaumont on the 22nd. Cliff's pop tour began on Wednesday, 9 November, at the Gaumont, Southampton, and

along the way it called at Birmingham, Middlesborough, Glasgow, Oxford, Croydon, Bournemouth, Manchester, Blackpool, Leicester, Southport and Southend, with a finale in aid of the Arts Centre Group at Watford on Monday, 12 December. Needless to say it was a sell-out, for hits or no hits the fans were still around in their thousands for the artiste who would be into his nineteenth year in show business by October.

Cliff was busy overseas as well as in Britain. He had a special Tear Fund concert in Rotterdam in October, preceded by a European tour from 1 to 26 September covering Finland, Sweden, Norway, Denmark, Germany, Holland, Austria, Belgium and France.

Europe's leading trade paper *Music Week* sent along Retailing Editor, Terri Anderson, to Cliff's 5 December concert at London's Royal Albert Hall. Her first reaction was how young he looked – not much more than eighteen was her initial reaction. 'He charmed the spots off everything in sight, and that included fans who were old enough to be his mother as well as young enough to be his daughters.' She thought the pervading atmosphere of the performance was one of 'brotherly informality' and was quick to add: 'It was never for a moment sloppy or off-hand. Neat and tight, clean and nice, and music, music, music.'

Terri ended her copy with: ' "Why Should the Devil Have All the Good Music" brought the whole evening to a family party climax, and the audience sang the lads off stage as white balloons floated from the ceiling. Showmanship – and a good voice. You really cannot knock it.'

The year had its usual assortment of specials and the odd quirks. The latter included his fan club's indecision as to what they could possibly buy him for his birthday! *Dynamite* noted: 'There will be no collection for Cliff this year, due to the problem that in the past years we did not know what to buy with the money, as Cliff is somebody who has nearly everything.' However, individual cards were suggested. His super-active fan following in the Portsmouth area via the Waterlooville Meeting House organized the Cliff Richard Birthday Disco with top Radio Victory DJ Glenn Richards running the turntables. They showed the film *A Day in the Life of Cliff Richard* and there was a buffet meal.

Cliff's Hong Kong friends celebrated his nineteenth show-business anniversary with the film *Take Me High* and sat back and watched the film *Wonderful Life* on television. And much happened elsewhere.

One of the year's specials was a media playback of *Every Face Tells a Story* at London's Carlton Tower Hotel. Cliff was there and so too was his friend and former Shadow man, producer Bruce Welch. Those who attended felt it was as good as anything Cliff had done and was a worthy follow-up to *I'm Nearly Famous*.

One of Cliff's more memorable personal happenings was finding himself stranded in New Zealand due to an airline dispute!

Particularly important in 1977 was a three-week visit to the States during June to promote the album *Every Face Tells a Story*.

Cliff's Mum stood in for him on 12 May at the Royal Garden Hotel, London, when The Shadows, after their concert at the Royal Albert Hall, received a number of gifts for sales of

their *Twenty Golden Greats* album.

Cliff's compilation album, *40 Golden Greats*, released in October, provided the big bonus event (apart from the tours) for fans in the year's last months. Cliff and management assembled at the Carlton Tower on 6 September for a pre-release ceremony. Bruce proposed they should also issue 40 Golden B-sides since he had written most of them! Germany announced they would make two changes to the album. 'Ready Teddy' and 'Spanish Harlem' were substituted for 'Gee Whizz It's You' and 'Constantly'. The album put Cliff into the top of the album charts.

At the Annual Music Therapy Silver Clef Luncheon on 18 October at the Café Royal in London it was announced that Cliff was the winner of the year's Silver Clef award for his services to the music industry. On the centenary celebration of the gramophone (not the magazine but the advent of the 'record player') and also the Queen's Silver Jubilee, the British Phonographic Industry gave its Britannia Award to Cliff as the Best British Male Solo Artist.

So 1977 was a mixed year, but 1978 promised much, for people were gearing themselves to celebrate twenty years of Cliff.

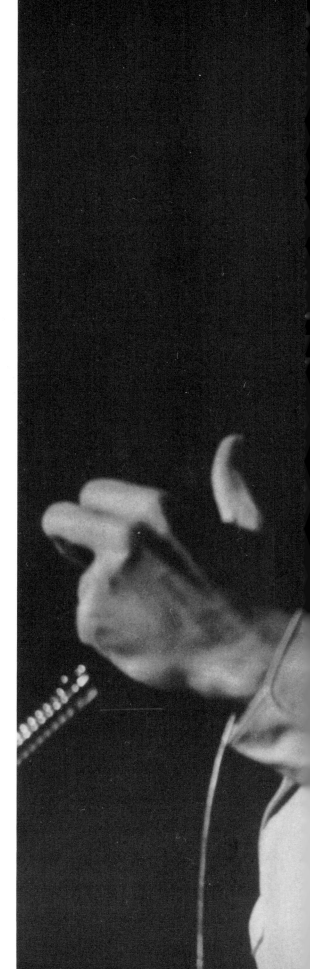

Tense moment during Cliff's performance at the Palladium, 1978

1977

On 8 August 1958 Cliff left Ferguson's and became a fully-fledged professional artiste. After twenty years in the business celebrations broke out everywhere. Magazines and newspapers vied for coverage.

The big happening for this twentieth year came months before the actual anniversary. From 27 February to 11 March the line-up of old was back again! Cliff and The Shadows were reunited after years for a series of concerts at the London Palladium. The posters stressed three elements: The Shadows, Cliff and his own band, and Cliff and The Shadows. Ticket prices were reasonable considering the importance of the occasion to thousands and thousands of fans, but then one of the unsung plus facts about Cliff is his low concert price structure which is usually well below that of many other artistes of similar standing. On this occasion tickets ranged from £2.50 to £6.50. Seats were sold out weeks before the show and, as might have been expected, the audience range was wide.

Some film clips began the evening's programme, then came Cliff and The Shadows for three songs – 'The Young Ones', 'Do You Wanna Dance' and 'The Day I Met Marie'. Cliff then left and The Shadows played through their hits, old and new. They closed the first half of the show with 'F.B.I.'

Cliff and his current band of musicians opened the second half with a new version of the old standard 'Please Don't Tease'. There was also more recent material as he sang two songs from *Small Corners*. He was showered with flowers and he looked sleek and slim in his white outfit trimmed with silver.

He also sang on his own, with one number, 'Melting Into One', guaranteed to bring tears to fans' eyes, but then came the moment which was really what the evening was about – Cliff and The Shadows reunited. There was a medley of old hits like 'Move It' and 'The Minute You're Gone' and there was 'Devil Woman', the big hit of 1976 which had revived Cliff's ailing chart fortunes.

For the show's finale everyone joined Cliff for a rousing 'Thank You Very Much'. Fans waved their arms, there were four encores and a

standing ovation, and then Cliff and the others were gone and the audience slowly made its way out into a cold winter's night.

There was another anniversary for Cliff in 1978 – ten years of Tear Fund and the Gospel concerts. It was in 1968 when Cliff and The Settlers strode the stage for the first Gospel concert which went under the title 'Help, Hope and Hallelujah'.

At the Royal Albert Hall in London on 9 and 10 October Cliff chatted with friend Bill Latham about Tear Fund and his faith. Seats here ranged from £1.00 to £3.50, with standing at 50p. Cliff talked of the latest Tear Fund projects. Garth Hewitt came on stage and spoke about his association in recent times with Tear Fund in Haiti. Dave Pope was next on stage to join Cliff and Garth singing a song Dave had written about his experiences entitled 'That's Why We're Here'.

A short interval passed and Cliff in black trousers, black leather waistcoat and bright yellow shirt came back on stage for songs like 'Yes He Lives', 'We Believe in Loving' and 'Joseph'. He sang 'Your Unworthy Servant' which he had written for the year's anniversary concerts, and in his finale included 'Why Should the Devil' and 'We're All One'. The house lights came on for all the performers and the audience to sing 'How Great Thou Art'. It was another landmark; few other stars, if any, have supported any kind of charity for so long and with such vigour.

The twentieth and tenth anniversary concerts shielded everyone from the cold chill which once more descended on Cliff's record career. This was a year in which three releases in a row failed to chart and there would have been a fourth but for the albums and singles charts being extended from fifty to one hundred and to seventy-five respectively nationally. The chart change meant that the album *Green Light*, released in October, slipped in at fifty-seven early in 1979 for three weeks. Like 1975, 1978 was a year without any hit singles, even of the lowest chart placing. The three 'misses' were 'Yes He Lives' (which seemed good enough), 'Please Remember Me' and the emotive 'Can't Take the Hurt Anymore'.

Nevertheless, the anniversary

celebrations made the year warm. As for Cliff himself and his twenty years: 'The years seemed to have slipped away without me even noticing . . . I can hardly believe it . . . I've really had a fantastic twenty years, and if it all ended for me tomorrow, I could never grumble, because I've had more than my fair share of show-business time. I mean I don't want it to end tomorrow, and I sincerely hope it doesn't. It's been a fantastic twenty years.

'People keep asking me how long I think it might go on. I suppose it's an attitude of mind. I mean I'd like it to go on, so that's a help. If I can maintain my voice, if I can keep it in tune, then I could still keep recording. Even if I had a voice to sing with in twenty years' time, if I didn't sing the right songs then I'm afraid I wouldn't deserve to have hits. So that would put the kybosh on it.

'I'm just looking forward to what the next five or six years have to hold. I feel much more excited about the *Green Light* album than I was about *Every Face Tells a Story*, or even *Small Corners*, which was one of the most

Brian, CR, Bruce and Hank celebrate the twentieth anniversary album with smiles all round

1978

Opposite: He may have been singing for twenty years but the enthusiasm and love for his singing career seem as fresh as ever

exciting things for me, because I've never produced one of my own albums before.'

Cliff said he was one of a long string of people who had looked for fame and fortune and found it insufficient. In a more frivolous moment he said his slimness was due to holding back on potatoes and bread but he had been known to reach for the odd bar of chocolate! He told the DJ Mike Reid that he had a love for shirts with some kind of special detail on them, perhaps edged in gold or silver, and he hated wearing ties. On another occasion he said: 'I've grown tired and wary of the hoary old questions about marriage which usually have some in-built innuendo about homosexuality.'

As for other people's comments, there was one from John Blake in the London *Evening News*, who said: 'Cliff is altogether too well scrubbed and asexually wholesome to be a real star.' Quite what 'real' meant must have puzzled many when considered against Cliff's twenty years of achievement.

As well as celebrations, there were the media activities, both general and Christian.

He was the star guest at the religious booksellers' convention at the Wembley Conference Centre on 31 January. He chatted about his biography and sang some songs. Also with Cliff were US singer Chuck Girard, and Roy Castle and wife Fiona. Cliff was a guest at Roy's Fairfield Hall concert in February which was in aid of the Arts Centre Group. In the same month he guested on *Pebble Mill* on BBC TV and talked about the album *Small Corners* and sang two songs.

During the first quarter of 1978 he also visited South Africa and Hong Kong. From South Africa an angry Cliff launched a tirade against BBC's Radio One for giving little time to his new single 'Yes He Lives'. He said: 'I hear that "Yes He Lives" was banned because of its religious connotations. If so, I find it most unfair.'

And while he was in this mood Cliff accused the television people of being unreceptive. 'I found a terrible insensitivity from them in their understanding of my own musical concepts.' And for good measure he hit out at the British musical press: 'cheap, infantile hostility' were the

words he used to describe their reaction to his work. But then British music was undergoing a considerable change and the advent of punk and new wave had caught the imagination of the music press.

Cliff gave three concerts in Hong Kong on 12, 13 and 14 May, which as usual were sell-outs, and 6-19 August was declared Cliff Richard Fortweek. He was interviewed and featured on numerous Continental programmes and his films and books seemed well to the fore.

Once more his British tour took place in the autumn and winter. The secular ran from the Odeon, Southampton, on 1 November to a finale at the Royal Albert Hall, London, on 11 December. A last-minute extra concert was added on 12 December at the Dominion Theatre, Tottenham Court Road, London. The concert linked to a Christmas effort for children organized by London's commercial radio station, Capital. Every person who came to Cliff's concert had to give a toy and the collected gifts would be given to underprivileged children. The secular tour was preceded by the Tear Fund Gospel tour which ran from 3 to 14 October though the dates were not consecutive.

There were a number of other Cliff charity events, apart from Tear Fund. One was a concert at the Ford Motor Company works theatre, near Brentwood, Essex, for Valerie Haddert. She was in her thirties and had been struck down with multiple sclerosis as a teenager. All tickets were sold at £5 and the full house was 250. Cliff had during his career read some of Valerie's poems on stage.

His religious activities continued. He made another appearance on stage with evangelist Dick Saunders at his London Crusade on 2 September. Cliff sang four songs and talked about his faith. He gave an interview for Australian TV on his Christian beliefs, and his religious autobiography re-appeared in a special pictorial edition with the text completely updated.

Radio One ran a five-part series on his career, beginning on 1 October, which was put together by Tim Rice.

Twenty years had passed and Cliff was still looking forward to more of the same!

1978

1979

That's me TJ with the maestro – now
what was the joke? My secret

The new year started badly but it ended in glory. This was the year when Cliff was reborn, musically. The growth has continued, proving to be quite unlike the 1976 promise which faded so abruptly after 'Devil Woman'.

Cliff's single, 'We Don't Talk Anymore', released in July, was the major factor in Cliff's rebirth. Apart from being a superb pop record and delighting all but hardened punksters and heavy metal addicts it gave Cliff his first number one in eleven years. That in itself was cause for celebration.

It was an almost unexpected event, for Cliff's first single of 1979 was 'Green Light' which, thanks to the chart being extended in length, only managed to crawl into a top placing of fifty-seven.

His second album of the year, *Rock 'n' Roll Juvenile*, confirmed even more clearly that he was back in business. But if the record hadn't triumphed, then more than likely Cliff would have called it a day and begun farewell tours. He knew deep down and admitted to me that to retain any credibility he had to compete and win against the best of the day. He couldn't continue with smallish selling records even if his lack of record success was balanced by an endless run of sell-out tours, TV and radio spots.

CLIFF DOES IT AGAIN shouted the Cliff Richard Fan Club of London. *Newsbeat* man of the time Richard Skinner was at the head of those who interviewed Cliff and asked him for his reaction. The response was predictable: 'It feels fantastic . . . it's just wonderful, I can't get over it.'

For the thousands at the Christian music-talk festival at Greenbelt near Bedford on 7 September the event couldn't have come at a better time for here was their star performer at the top of the pop chart. And by good fortune it was the year Radio One had arranged to be there for a special programme!

Oddly, Cliff was not at his best at the 1979 Greenbelt festival. His band was minus two regulars and seemed to go a little astray at times, but for all that he was very much the star attraction. He sang 'We Don't Talk Anymore', and 'Yes He Lives' was another highlight. He closed with 'Why Should the Devil Have All the Good Music'.

It was an exciting late summer and early autumn. However, much had happened in the normal run of things before the dramatic success of the hit single and Christian rock festival.

In February the reunion of Cliff and The Shadows appeared on the album *Thank You Very Much*, and in the Netherlands EMI Holland reissued nine Cliff albums. Collectors from everywhere chased the lists and records. Cliff was in South Africa once more in February, and in May he appeared for a fortnight at London's

1979

Palladium with Skyband and special guests Bryn Haworth and Jackie Beason. The Nigel Lythgoe Dancers also performed. Indeed Cliff danced with them and did a routine based on 'Hot Shot', which was to be the single release following 'We Don't Talk Anymore'. Cliff pays tribute to Elton in the lyrics of 'Hot Shot'. 'Thank You Very Much' closed the show and the audience waved their arms in the air in the traditional way.

EMI threw a special luncheon for Cliff in February to celebrate their twenty-one years together. Managing Director Bob Mercer presented Cliff with a gold replica of the key to EMI's Manchester Square headquarters in London. In addition, Cliff and The Shadows were presented with framed prints of three cricket bats shadowed against a wall, parodying their original *20 Golden Greats* sleeve design of three guitar necks. As *Dynamite* reported in its usual informative manner, the boys received a standing ovation.

Cliff also attended the annual dinner of Europe's leading trade journal *Music Week* where awards came his and The Shadows' way once more.

The 1979 European tour from 2 to 23 October took in twenty-two concerts in twenty-three days, preceding a seven-week tour of Britain from 1 November to 18 December. And news of Cliff's role as a producer for Garth Hewitt on the album *Did He Jump . . . Or Was He Pushed?* received considerable publicity.

There was an interesting transition for Cliff when he made some appearances at London churches soon after his Palladium season in May. Among the churches were St Mary's, Islington, and Holy Trinity, Brompton. As usual Bill Latham was there as well and Cliff answered questions, talked about his faith and sang some songs. He wore a blue and white jacket with a badge proclaiming 'Yes He Lives'. Cliff said rock 'n' roll came a poor second to Jesus and that being a Christian was the most important part of his life. He also visited Billericay Baptist Church in Essex and shared in the service of baptism for backing group member Stu Calver and wife Lyn. Cliff spoke after the service, talking of his own faith and his joy at being baptized as an adult.

Cliff also appeared in *Startalk* at the Royal Court Theatre, Liverpool, on 10 June and talked for some one and a quarter hours about his music and views on life. He sang five songs, a mix of secular and religious. Cliff praised some elements of recent music and singled out for praise a rock band with Christian roots called After the Fire.

He was at the gathering of the European Baptist Federation in Brighton at the end of June. Cliff had members of the Russian Baptist Church in his audience as he told of his visit to the USSR and sang several songs. He also mentioned Bangladesh and sang, among other songs, his own composition 'Moving Along'. His set ended with 'When I Survey the Wondrous Cross'.

In September Cliff travelled the length and breadth of Britain promoting *Rock 'n' Roll Juvenile*. He appeared on major radio and TV shows as well as talking with endless press people. He brought London's famous Oxford Street to a standstill when he signed copies of his album at the HMV Shop near Bond Street underground station. He did a special signing session at the Record Scene, Ashford, which under John Friesen's drive and inspiration has become the world's number one shop for Cliff and Shadows material.

The European and UK tours followed with Cliff appearing in red satin shirt, black leather trousers and black jacket with red guitars on the lapels and the back of the jacket. During the second half of the show Cliff wore 1950s baggy trousers and embroidered shirt.

In December he took part in a major concert in Camberley, Surrey, to aid the International Year of the Child and he joined a crowd of 30,000 outside Buckingham Palace for carol singing on 16 December. Two days later, in Coventry, Cliff gave a concert in aid of the Arts Centre Group. It could hardly exist without his generosity in money and time.

Before the twelve days of Christmas were over Cliff was busy at work once more, bound for America on 31 December. There's no rest when you're a star of his calibre and have hit the number one spot after eleven years!

Opposite: He's quite entitled to smile – thanks to his first chart-topper since 1968 with 'We Don't Talk Anymore'

1979

Opposite: Janet Johnson with daughter Marianne at Cliff's London office. Cliff waves cheques from the London Fan Club for Tear Fund

Could it really be true that he was forty? It was the event that captured the press in 1980 but hardly excited Cliff. The man in question said with due nonchalance: 'I've reached it without noticing. To me it's just another birthday.'

He was more delighted with his receipt of an OBE. He was certainly more forthcoming: 'It's fantastic – it's marvellous.' He turned up at Buckingham Palace on 23 July for his date with the Queen attired in a black lounge suit set off by bright red training-style shoes and blending tie, a rose in his buttonhole.

Pop fans, the music business, religious leaders, and mums and dads said he deserved the award. He was joined for the occasion by his Mum Dorothy Bodkin who said it was 'fantastic'. Afterwards the Webbs celebrated.

As far as his birthday was concerned, the *Daily Mirror* thought it time to tell everybody that he was as youthful as ever. Elsewhere he was described as young and fresh as a choirboy, and labelled the 'golden oldie' and the 'Peter Pan' of pop.

He had his birthday right in the middle of his extraordinary three-week season at London's Apollo Theatre, Victoria. After the show on 14 October there was a private dinner party for family and friends closest to him.

He told Pauline McLeod of the *Mirror* he had three ambitions: first, to be involved in a stage version of a rock-and-roll musical; second, to be a major US star; and third, to have a wife and children. On the latter he stressed that the 'right girl' was important.

EMI issued Cliff facts – seventy-five hits, ten number one's, more than 1,000 weeks in the charts – while in other quarters enquirers after his secret of youth were told by Cliff: 'I make sure I take vitamin capsules, which include vitamins B, C, E and ginseng every day. And when I'm not working I make sure I swim as often as I can. It's very important for me to be strict with myself because in the pop world there are a lot of weird hours and a temptation to all kinds of excesses.'

The concert reviews for his amazing three-week season at the Victoria Apollo were good. Derek Jewell in the *Sunday Times* commented that Cliff had improved with the years, even if he was not the writer's kind of singer. He thought the newer songs were perhaps the best he had ever sung.

Janet Johnson in *Dynamite* proclaimed: 'It was really an emotional sight, a perfect and superb show. Cliff is amazing – his career spans two decades (three actually) and yet he remains fresh, younger looking, up-to-date and above all – a STAR. . .

'I think we've backed a winner don't you????'

Cliff was dressed in an apple-green outfit for half the occasion. He had another outfit for the second half of the show – glittery shirt and shiny black pants and those now-famous red trainers on his feet. Janet Johnson sat there and wondered where Cliff found all his energy!

Olivia Newton-John made an appearance of sorts. Cliff sang his hit song from the film *Xanadu*, a duet with Olivia entitled 'Suddenly'. For this a curtain was lowered and a giant heart appeared on to which were projected pictures of the lady who had first found her musical feet while singing on Cliff's TV shows in the early 1970s.

There was much else happening for Cliff. His singles fared extremely well. 'Carrie' went to number four, 'Dreamin'' reached the top ten, and 'Suddenly' (with Olivia Newton-John) reached number fifteen. The 1980 album was *I'm No Hero*. The reviews were great.

The year had begun with another Cliff media assault on the United States. The promotional tour went with his big UK comeback single 'We Don't Talk Anymore'. Cliff appeared on the *Dinah Shore Show* and also another top-rated chat programme, the *Mike Douglas Show*. For Miss Shore Cliff had to explain what the letters OBE meant. On the *Mike Douglas Show* it was Cliff the big British hit-maker, secure in the knowledge that 'We Don't Talk Anymore' was in the Stateside top ten. Of his visit in 1960 Cliff, now twenty years older, told Douglas: 'In 1960 I came over and was added on a fantastic string of people like Frankie Avalon, Clovers Crest, Freddie Cannon, Bobby Rydell, and we were the added attraction from Great Britain, and when we stopped the show at night

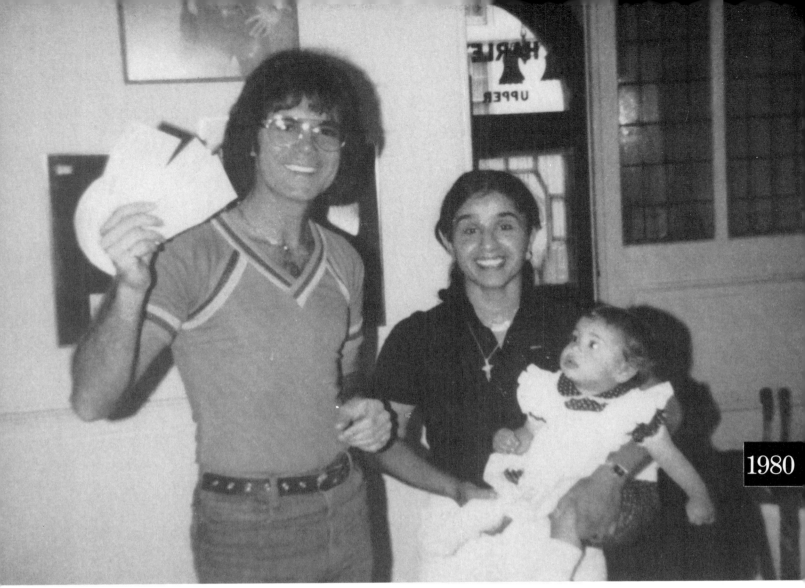

1980

we thought we'd won America, but you need a machine over here, this place is so big.'

In March Cliff returned for another major US chat TV show, this time the *Merv Griffin Show*. 'Carrie' was now the single running up the US charts and he had a new album out in America entitled *We Don't Talk Anymore*.

Griffin in wonderment exclaimed: 'You date back to 1960?'

Cliff: 'I go back even further!'

Griffin talked of his incredible career, of Cliff the reborn Christian, and Cliff filled in with relevant material as well as telling of the European middle-of-the-road years in his life.

While in America he also appeared on a *Midnight Special* TV show with Olivia Newton-John. There was some friendly banter and then the two sang 'Suddenly'.

He had another tour in South

Africa which began in the later part of February and ran into the second week of March with concerts in Durban, Port Elizabeth, Cape Town and Johannesburg. Two concerts planned for Bobhuthatswana and Klerksdorp were cancelled due to segregation problems. In Johannesburg he had support from local band Backtrax. Cliff sang a total of nineteen songs. The audience joined him, at his invitation, in singing 'Summer Holiday' and 'Living Doll'. While he was in South Africa he heard he had been awarded the BBC TV *Nationwide-Daily Mirror-BBC Radio One* Golden Award as Best Family Entertainer. A telephone link between Cliff and Tim Rice was arranged for the presentation.

In May and early June he was recording in Germany, where he was also filming for German TV. A German concert tour was pencilled in for three weeks in September, as was

another South African visit in November, this time a Gospel tour along with Garth Hewitt.

A lunch with Cliff was the prize offered to the highest bidder by London's Capital Radio in April as part of their Help a London Child campaign. Mrs Kim Kayne, wife of a property developer, bid £1,400 and won the lunch with Cliff. She said it was a wonderful experience.

In the early part of the summer Cliff took a well-deserved holiday, but even if he was silent his momentum continued worldwide in TV and radio programming, a fact of life whatever the time of year. Dutch TV showed Cliff at the Palladium, Australia saw Cliff and Olivia Newton-John on a special *Hollywood Nights* TV show, New Zealand saw Cliff in the BBC programme *Thank You Very Much*, and many countries broadcast Cliff's appearances on the Kenny Everett TV programme. Many throughout the world heard his series of Monday programmes entitled *Reflections* on the World Service of the BBC.

In the autumn Cliff was spotted a few times with Olivia Newton-John who accompanied him when he appeared at an ITN TV silver anniversary party.

A new book by Cliff entitled *Happy Christmas from Cliff* appeared on the bookstands. It was bright and cheery, had numerous new photos, features and puzzles. It sold for £3.50.

He signed once more with EMI for worldwide distribution and had his photograph taken by Lord Snowdon as part of the International Year of Disabled People appeal. Apparently the Lord wasn't too taken with Cliff's shirt and suggested Cliff wore one of his. After a quick rummage through a cupboard Lord Snowdon drew out a pale blue one.

There was just one sad note in the year when he attended a special memorial concert to his long-time record producer Norrie Paramor at the Fairfield Hall, Croydon, on 6 February. Norrie had died the previous year. The concert was in aid of the Stars Organization for Spastics with Her Royal Highness, The Duchess of Kent, the principal guest. Cliff topped the artiste bill and he was accompanied by the Ron Goodwin Orchestra. He sang six numbers, all of them recalling the Cliff-Norrie success story. Cliff told of how the two had worked together for fifteen years and of all the record success they had had. He gave a short speech praising Norrie Paramor, who was recalled as a conductor, composer, arranger, pianist and producer. He had his own unique 'Norrie Paramor' sound and of course produced other artistes than Cliff and had records issued under his own name. As the magazine *The Christian Friends of Cliff* said: 'All honour to his memory.'

This was another successful year though without extensive Gospel and secular tours. It was the year of Cliff Richard OBE, concerts for three weeks at the Victoria Apollo, and of course his fortieth birthday.

With Michael Aspel for his Capital Radio show, London. Left is former manager Tito Burns

1980

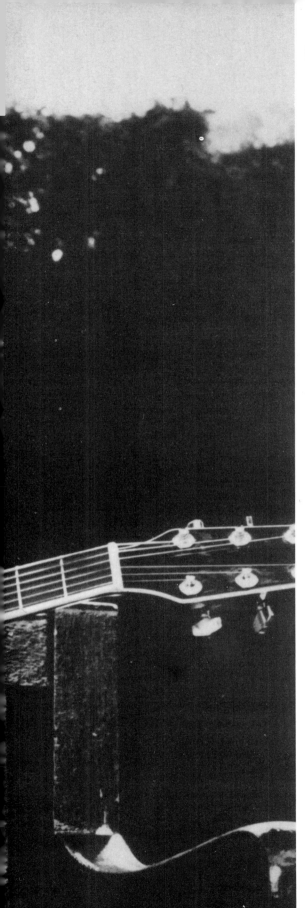

1981

Opposite: Hits and good days lie in the past but there are chart successes and moments to treasure yet to be added to his story

This was to be a Cliff TV year, one in which BBC 2, in co-operation with Lella Productions, producer Norman Stone and his multi-talented team, did Cliff proud.

He muttered: 'I would say that I've never been as excited about a TV show of mine for a long, long time and I've got great faith in it.'

Documentary and light entertainment techniques were carefully woven together, with each of the four fifty-minute programmes tackling a different angle in the life and make-up of Cliff. *Rock 'n' Roll Juvenile*, the first programme, concentrated on Cliff's long-running pop career. The second programme centred on Cliff's Gospel activities and took in some film from a recent tour. It was titled after the song Cliff had been singing for several years, *Why Should the Devil Have All the Good Music*. The third programme, *Travellin' Light*, caught Cliff on the road in America, the area where one of his unresolved ambitions lay. Programme four was *My Kinda Life*, forty-year-old Cliff, the private and public personality.

The first appeared on Monday, 23 November, with the others on the following three Mondays. And to put the gilt on the gingerbread there was an *Everyman* TV special on Cliff on Boxing Day. *Everyman* dealt with Cliff the man of faith, his beliefs and views.

While the TV screens brought Cliff into thousands of homes he hit number two on the singles chart with 'Daddy's Home' from his major chart hit album *Wired for Sound*. Also faring well was the first hardback on Cliff since David Winter's volume

published in the late 1960s. It was written by ex-*Mirror* Features Editor, Pat Doncaster, and this writer.

In 1981 Cliff was the superstar, Britain's number one, living up to all the superlatives. And to think he was forty-one! It seemed ridiculous.

Before the TV explosion there was a British tour running from 2 November until 19 December. Cliff did something different and special. He stayed for four nights in eight locations. These favoured places were Glasgow, Edinburgh, Manchester, Brighton, Birmingham, London, Bournemouth and deep down in the West Country, St Austell in Cornwall.

The year began the way it ended, with endless Cliff activity. December 1980 had seen the release in the US of the single 'Little in Love' coupled with 'Everyman'. In Britain, after some delay and remixing, 'Little in Love' was issued in February, with 'Keep on Looking' replacing the US B side. Cliff was in the States in early January promoting his single and album, *I'm No Hero*, returning in time to attend on 16 January at the Royal Albert Hall the 25th Anniversary Rally of the monthly Christian journal *Crusade* of which Cliff's friend David Winter had for some years been editor. Billy Graham was featured as well. Cliff talked of his recent visits to South Africa and the States and sang three songs, 'You and Me Jesus', 'Lord I Love You' and 'Moving In'.

There was also the promised Gospel tour which kicked off in Dublin on 19 January. The first British date was 23 January in Exeter

Opposite: The publicity shot which was circulated amongst media people to promote his major TV series in 1981

with the final one at the ABC Theatre, Peterborough, on 2 February. The tour raised around £50,000 for Tear Fund and was particularly exciting on the musical level for the number of new songs which made their appearance. British writers David Cooke, Chris Eaton and John Daniels provided some of the material. The group Network 3 were also on the bill. Cliff went through various sets of clothes and enraptured his audiences with his general vocal presentation.

During his concert in Sheffield on 5 February the major German magazine *Bravo for Cliff* named him their choice as Top International Male Singer and made a presentation.

Cliff appeared on the long-running top-rated BBC TV programme, the *Michael Parkinson Show*, on 28 March during which he sang 'Heartbreak Hotel' and accompanied himself on guitar.

And then it was America and Canada once more for a tour which opened in Seattle, Washington State, on 3 March and ended on 18 April. The tour covered thousands and thousands of miles with Cliff calling at such US cities as New York, Philadelphia, Cleveland and Los Angeles, and Victoria, Vancouver, Calgary, Edmonton, Saskatoon and Winnipeg in Canada. He wore black leather trousers, a black shirt with gold trim, red leather jacket and red shoes. There was a red belt for extra effect. The music was gutsy, perhaps in parts more rock-based than most of his output in Britain. Flowers, gold jewellery, even stuffed animals came his way from appreciative members of the fast growing Stateside fan following. Oddly enough audiences resembled British ones in that the age range was from the pre-teens to the over sixties.

Olivia Newton-John appeared at his New York gig, as did Bill Latham and Cliff's Mum. It was more of a night-club-style atmosphere with everyone seated at tables and drinks being served throughout.

After seven weeks away Cliff returned to Britain for some very special events which were in part related to his forthcoming television shows.

There was a Cliff Richard special on 1 May at London's Hammersmith Odeon. All those attending were requested to wear 1950s clothing. Two days later a wig-wearing, old-style greasy-look Cliff was filmed at the Hard Rock Café near Hyde Park Corner. The Teddy Boy Cliff wore black leather drainpipes, lurex tie, crepe shoes and white jacket. He was filmed singing 'D in Love' and was backed by a youthful Shadows of the 1980s, The Fantoms.

The summer saw Cliff taking some time off in his old haunt, Portugal. On 13 August there was a one-off concert in Bophuthatswana, South Africa, where he appeared wearing red shorts! During the second half his shorts were replaced by black leather wet-look trousers, red leather wet-look jacket and gold-trimmed black shirt. His encore was 'Sing a Song of Freedom', now no longer banned.

On 24 July he was spotted in Milton Keynes filming promotional material for the autumn album *Wired for Sound*. Alan Tarney was once more named as producer. Those who heard advance plays pronounced it full of hit singles, which proved to be true enough.

Meantime Cliff and Garth Hewitt aided Youth for Christ in Holland and Cliff appeared at Greenbelt on 30 August. A few days later he gave two concerts at the Wembley Conference Centre for the Arts Centre Group as it celebrated its tenth birthday. Garth Hewitt and Network 3 joined Cliff. The shows ended with Garth's song 'The One for All'.

The *Daily Mirror*'s British Rock and Pop Awards nominated Cliff as the Best Male Singer. The Stringfellows club in London sold a Cliff Richard drink at £2.50 (it comprised lemon juice, pineapple juice, grenadine, egg white, lemonade, and fresh fruit for decoration). Cliff attended the wedding of Steve Turner, poet and rock journalist, to Mo McCafferty of Network 3 at Westminster Chapel on 27 June. Members of the International Cliff Richard Movement voted 'We Don't Talk Anymore' their all-time favourite Cliff song.

During Wimbledon in late June/early July Cliff was heard speaking with Betsy Nagelsen during the radio commentary. Cliff said he didn't play enough tennis. But 1982 would correct that. . .

1981

1982

For the media it was the game of the year – Cliff Richard and Sue Barker. Were they more than just good friends? Could they be in love? Would they become engaged? Might they even marry?

The two were frequently seen together – on the tennis court, at the airport, even on the first night of the Rudolf Nureyev ballet at the London Coliseum Theatre.

Cliff joked: 'Someone has to take over from Charles and Di!' while from time to time both commented on their relationship which at one point so satisfied Sue that she exclaimed: 'Just say I'm a very lucky and very happy girl.'

There were those who thought the couple should be left alone. Some of the Christian press said so.

Cliff's fans were agog. It seemed to be their hero's first real love affair since perhaps Olivia Newton-John, or even as far back as Jackie Irving. Sue was a Christian and the press made sure everyone was aware of the fact. Britain's leading youth-orientated religious journal *Buzz* said there was an unwritten agreement among Christian media not to spill the beans about prominent conversions let alone become involved in any love-match.

Buzz said: 'Within two weeks of that [Cliff telling Arts Centre Group members that Sue had become a Christian convert] the *Sunday Mirror* ran the story of Sue's conversion and the "sensitive" Christian media had been upstaged in trying to do the honourable thing.' However, soon there was a lengthy feature on convert Sue in *Today* (formerly *Crusade*) and the news was for all.

Dynamite, the magazine of the International Cliff Richard Movement, reported Cliff's annoyance over the release of 'Anyone for Tennis' by Paul Trevillion and Sadie Nine on Service Records. The press release accompanying it commented: 'On the record, Cliff and Sue can be heard enjoying a heated game of tennis complete with grunts and groans, but there is no "Love-All" ending.' The record disappeared without trace.

Whatever the pros and cons of their relationship, of Sue's conversion, of the general media and its handling of the whole affair, it was all pleasant enough when placed against two other 'love' stories which were attracting attention.

On 15, 16 and 17 February the *Daily Star* published the revelations of Carol Costa, ex-wife of Jet Harris, a former Shadow. She said Cliff had been her man and passion was the order of their relationship. When the story ran in the British newspaper Cliff was in Thailand; however, he told the *Daily Star* in Bangkok: 'My conversion to Christianity changed my attitude to morals.' He refused to comment on whether or not he had been involved with her at the time.

The other story suggested he might be having an affair with the extremely attractive wife of Rick Parfitt, the famed Status Quo group member. The suggestion was denied, not without some distaste. Certainly the two had been seen together but then both Parfitts had become increasingly concerned with Christian affairs. And Cliff was one of the witness team.

While the stories circulated, Cliff was busy furthering his pop career. It was an extremely busy year with a great deal of time spent overseas; however there were some events at home.

Early in January Cliff gave a concert at Skindles, Maidenhead, in aid of Yeldall Manor, a rehabilitation centre for drug and alcohol dependants.

The first week in February was spent at the Blazer's Club in Windsor. He introduced the concerts with 'Welcome to the first week of our world tour', and he told the audience how he would visit Hong Kong, Bangkok, Singapore, Australia, New Zealand, Scandinavia and Europe, plus the United States, before the year's end. Blazer's provided the setting for Cliff and band to try out their world tour musical set.

Cliff's Far East tour began in Hong Kong on 12 February. It had been forty-four months since his last visit in June 1978. He stayed at the new Holiday Inn and managed to find time for some shopping with other members of his entourage. His three concerts took place at the Queen Elizabeth Stadium which has seating capacity for 2,100 people. He took the stage at 20.15 hours and with artificial smoke swirling round he emerged singing 'Song of Thunder'. Other numbers included 'We Don't Talk Anymore', 'Move It', 'Broken Doll' and 'Dreamin''. He attended a special

Opposite: Sue and Cliff, Cliff and Sue – for a while it was all the newspapers talked about. This was taken at the Kensington Royal Garden Hotel, London

1982

party given by the Hong Kong branch of the International Cliff Richard Movement.

He left Hong Kong for Bangkok on Valentine's Day. A concert set for Kuala Lumpur, Malaysia, was cancelled. By 22 February he was in Australia and opened his short visit at the Entertainment Centre, Perth. He dressed in gold and black, a contrast from the overriding green colour of his clothing in Hong Kong and the dates immediately following.

During his time in Brisbane Cliff met a young girl called Rachel Scriven. She had undergone major eye surgery but seemingly to no avail and one of her wishes was to see Cliff in action before losing her sight. ICRM members met him at all concert locations in both Australia and New Zealand. Various New Zealand radio stations organized special travel parties for fans who did not live in the two city venues of Christchurch and Auckland.

In March Cliff was in Los Angeles for two important concerts in his effort to establish himself more firmly in America. He appeared on the major US TV show *Solid Gold*, and at the concerts and on TV he plugged his major American hit, 'Daddy's Home'. The concerts were held at the open-air 5,000-seat Greek Theatre.

Cliff played the Greek Theatre, Los Angeles, once more in July and also The Concord, San Francisco (the latter was a rather low-key affair with a small audience). Cliff then moved up into Canada and began a tour across the nation with dates in Toronto, Ottawa and Montreal.

Greenbelt was one British festival which he played in the late summer before appearing on a number of European TV specials. His Continental tour opened in Hannover on 10 October and ended in Cologne on 2 November. Cliff visited Berlin, Hamburg, Aarchus, Aalbourg, Helsinki, Oslo, Copenhagen, Rotterdam, Essen, Mannheim, Frankfurt, Munich, Brussels, Dusseldorf and Munster.

A month after the European tour was completed it was time for the British Gospel tour during which he visited Glasgow, Edinburgh, Bradford, Preston, Stoke-on-Trent, Wells, Hull, Cardiff, Swindon and Brighton. The Gospel tour ended on 18 December.

Earlier Christian activities included a week in Kenya in May with some concerts for charity and the making of a film strip for Tear Fund.

Cliff was featured on the first single from Rick Parfitt's wife Marietta, issued by Polydor and entitled 'You're Only Lonely' coupled with 'Making Up My Mind'. Cliff also sang back-ups with Kevin Godley, former 10CC member and now one half of Godley-Creme. EMI reissued twelve of Cliff's singles, including 'We Don't Talk Anymore' which had not, in fact, been deleted.

Readers of *TV Times* voted Cliff Top Singer of 1981. Ampex presented their Golden Reel Award to Cliff for his best-selling *Wired for Sound* which was recorded and mixed on an Ampex 465 tape. The company donated $1,000 to a charity nominated by Cliff – in this instance the Arts Centre Group.

Network 3, a group which Cliff had helped, folded. 'Daddy's Home' was voted by *Dynamite* readers their favourite Cliff song of all time. The previous number one, 'We Don't Talk Anymore', slipped to number three, but still in second position was 'Miss You Nights'. Cliff sang vocal harmony on B.A. Robertson's album *R+BA* and produced the Sheila Walsh single 'Star Song'. Cliff's co-producer on the August-released album *Now You See Me, Now You Don't*, Craig Prues, had his own single released by EMI. Olivia Newton-John told her career story at the Canadian National Exhibition and stressed the importance of Cliff in the early days of her career.

In October Cliff visited Finland for the first time in thirteen years. Before his concert in the 6,000-seat Helsinki Ice Stadium (all tickets sold) he was presented with sauna brushes and slippers by fan club members of the ICRM. Cliff arrived on 15 October and left on the 17th. One familiar face at Helsinki airport was the London Cliff Richard Fan Club President Janet Johnson who had arrived just a few minutes before Cliff.

As part of their fiftieth anniversary the London Philharmonic Orchestra presented 'An Evening with Cliff Richard and the LPO' in aid of their national appeal fund. The event was held on 23 November. Cliff appeared with his group and full orchestra for the second half of the concert. In Cliff's backing group was newcomer Terry Harding. Cliff told the audience the LPO was the only group which had lasted longer than his!

He featured some newish concert material, including 'True Love Ways', 'Treasure of Love', 'One in a Million' and 'Up in the World', plus of course familiars like 'Daddy's Home', 'Miss You Nights', 'Devil Woman', 'Green Light', 'We Don't Talk Anymore' and his latest single 'Little Town'.

The flip side of 'Little Town' featured two of Cliff's compositions. 'Love and a Helping Hand' was from the new Tear Fund film *Cliff in Kenya* and the other was 'You, Me and Jesus'. The film was scheduled for showing during the Garth Hewitt Tear Fund tour of 1983.

For Cliff the year ended in a joyous manner. His 'Little Town' made the top twenty. He said: 'If you know Jesus then you know the peace of Christmas.' He told his fans, 'Have a peace-filled time!'

The Christian record star had a hit record and he was telling a story precious to him. It was the best of both worlds. And while he enjoyed a peaceful Christmas and New Year there was activity already being planned elsewhere; after all, 1983 was Silver Jubilee Year!

Cliff with one of pop's most prolific and most respected journalists, the late Dick Tatham

1982

This is the year when everyone is saying 'congratulations' to Cliff, which makes a change from him singing it! It is his silver anniversary in the music business. It will be 1987 before Paul McCartney can celebrate his quarter century of hit records, and 1988 for The Rolling Stones – assuming they are still performing and making records then.

At the outset of silver anniversary year things were already hectic with massive tours arranged and many activities being planned. Given the printing schedule for this book, the year can be only briefly outlined, but the early signs indicated that it was going to be another 'wonderful' year.

Cliff played Blazer's Night Club in Windsor from 20 to 26 January. Tickets were priced £22.50.

In February he joined Phil Everly on a Capitol-issued single 'She Means Nothing to Me'. He also lent vocal aid to Phil for his solo album.

His tour dates for the first half of the year were as follows:

FEBRUARY
2-3	Singapore
6-7	Bangkok
9-11	Hong Kong
13-15	Manila

APRIL
9	Lisbon, Portugal
13	Barcelona, Spain
15	Stuttgart, Germany
16	HOF, Germany
19	Essen, Germany
20	Siegen, Germany
22	Malmo, Sweden
23	Gothenburg, Sweden
26	Rotterdam, Holland
27	Antwerp, Holland
28	Brussels, Belgium
30	Manchester Apollo, England

Early November sees Cliff opening another five-week season at the Apollo Theatre, Victoria, London.

This is how EMI saw Cliff in early 1983

1983

UK RECORD RELEASES

All albums listed were released by EMI. Where both sides of a single were listed separately in the charts, the position of each is given in brackets after the title. In all other cases except one the number in brackets refers to the first title – the A side. The exception is 'Move It', originally released as a B side in 1958, which reached number two in the charts.

1957/8

SINGLES

Schoolboy Crush/Move It (2). Columbia DB 4178. August. Also 78 r.p.m. release.

High Class Baby/My Feet Hit the Ground. (7). Columbia DB 4203. November. Also 78 r.p.m. release.

1959

SINGLES

Livin' Lovin' Doll/Steady With You. (20). Columbia DB 4249. January. Also 78 r.p.m. release.

Mean Streak (10)/Never Mind (21). Columbia DB 4290. April. Also 78 r.p.m. release.

Living Doll/Apron Strings. (1). Columbia DB 4306. July. Re-entered charts December (26) and again January 1960 (28). Also 78 r.p.m. release.

Travellin' Light (1)/Dynamite (16). Columbia DB 4351. October. Also 78 r.p.m. release.

EPs

Serious Charge: Living Doll/No Turning Back/Mad About You/Chinchilla (The Shadows). May.

Cliff No. 1: Apron Strings/My Babe/Down the Line/I Gotta Feeling/Baby I Don't Care. June.

Cliff No. 2: Donna/Move It/Ready Teddy/Too Much/Don't Bug Me Baby. July.

ALBUMS

Cliff: Apron Strings/My Babe/Down the Line/I Got a Feeling/Jet Black (The Drifters)/Baby I Don't Care/Donna/Move It/Ready Teddy/Too Much/Don't Bug Me Baby/Driftin' (The Drifters)/That'll Be the Day/Be-Bop-A-Lula (The Drifters)/Danny/Whole Lotta Shakin' Goin' On. Mono SX 1147. April.

Cliff Sings: Blue Suede Shoes/The Snake and the Bookworm/I Gotta Know/Here Comes Summer/I'll String Along With You/Embraceable You/As Time Goes By/The Touch of Your Lips/Twenty Flight Rock/Pointed Toe Shoes/Mean Woman Blues/I'm Walkin'/I Don't Know Why/Little Things Mean a Lot/Somewhere Along the Way/That's My Desire. Mono SX 1192. November.

1960

SINGLES

Voice in the Wilderness/Don't Be Mad at Me. (2). Columbia DB 4398. January. Re-entered charts May (36). Also 78 r.p.m. release.

Fall in Love With You/Willie and the Hand Jive. (2). Columbia DB 4431. March.

Please Don't Tease/Where Is My Heart. (1). Columbia DB 4479. June.

Nine Times Out of Ten/Thinking of Our Love. (3). Columbia DB 4506. September.

I Love You/'D' in Love. (1). Columbia DB 4547. December.

EPs

Expresso Bongo: Love/A Voice in the Wilderness/The Shrine on the Second Floor/Bongo Blues (The Shadows). (24). January.

Cliff Sings No. 1: Here Comes Summer/I Gotta Know/Blue Suede Shoes/The Snake and the Bookworm. February.

Cliff Sings No. 2: Twenty Flight Rock/Pointed Toe Shoes/Mean Woman Blues/I'm Walkin'. March.

Cliff Sings No. 3: I'll String Along With You/Embraceable You/As Time Goes By/The Touch of Your Lips. June.

Cliff Sings No. 4: I Don't Know Why (I Just Do)/Little Things Mean a Lot/Somewhere Along the Way/That's My Desire. September.

Cliff's Silver Discs: Please Don't Tease/Fall in Love With You/Nine Times Out of Ten/Travellin' Light. December.

ALBUMS

Me and My Shadows: I'm Gonna Get You/You and I/I Cannot Find a True Love/Evergreen Tree/She's Gone/Left Out Again/You're Just the One to Do It/Lamp of Love/Choppin' 'n' Changin'/We Have It Made/Tell Me/Gee Whizz It's You/I Love You So/I'm Willing to Learn/I Don't Know/Working After School. Mono SX 1261, stereo SCX 3330, different takes. October.

1961

SINGLES

Theme For a Dream/Mumblin' Mosie. (4). Columbia DB 4593. February.

Gee Whizz It's You/I Cannot Find a True Love (export single). (4). Columbia DC 756. March. Demand in the UK for this export single was such that it reached no. 4 in the UK charts.

A Girl Like You/Now's the Time to Fall in Love. (3). Columbia DB 4667. June.

When the Girl in Your Arms Is the Girl in Your Heart/Got a Funny Feeling. (3). Columbia DB 4716. October.

EPs

Me and My Shadows No. 1: I'm Gonna Get You/You and I/I Cannot Find a True Love/Evergreen Tree/She's Gone. February.

Me and My Shadows No. 2: Left Out Again/You're Just the One to Do It/Lamp of Love/Choppin' 'n' Changin'/We Have Made It. March.

Me and My Shadows No. 3: Tell Me/Gee Whizz It's You/I'm Willing to Learn/I Love You So/I Don't Know. April.

Listen to Cliff No 1: What'd I Say/True Love Will Come to You/Blue Moon/Lover. October.

Dream: Dream/All I Do Is Dream of You/I'll See You in My Dreams/When I Grow Too Old to Dream. November.

Listen to Cliff No. 2: Unchained Melody/First Lesson in Love/Idle Gossip/Almost Like Being in Love/Beat Out Dat Rhythm on a Drum. December.

ALBUMS

Listen to Cliff: What'd I Say/Blue Moon/Trust Love Will Come to You Lover/Unchained Melody/Idle Gossip/First Lesson in Love/Almost Like Being in Love/Beat Out Dat Rhythm on a Drum/Memories Linger On/Temptation/I Live For You/Sentimental Journey/I Want You to Know/We Kiss in a Shadow/It's You. Mono SX 1320, stereo SCX 3375, different takes. May.

21 Today: Happy Birthday to You/Forty Days/Catch Me/How Wonderful to Know/Tough Enough/Fifty Tears for Every Kiss/The Night Is So Lonely/Poor Boy/Y' Arriva/Outsider/Tea For Two/To Prove My Love For You/Without You/A Mighty Lonely Man/My Blue Heaven/Shame On You. Mono SX 1368, stereo SCX 3409. October.

The Young Ones: Friday Night/Got a Funny Feeling/Peace Pipe/Nothing's Impossible/The Young Ones/All for One/Lessons in Love/No One for Me But Nicky/What D'You Know We've Got a Show and Vaudeville Routine/When the Girl in Your Arms Is the Girl in Your Heart/Just Dance/Mood Mambo/The Savage/We Say Yeah. Mono SX 1384, stereo SCX 3397. December.

1962

SINGLES

The Young Ones/We Say Yeah. (1). Columbia DB 4761. January.

I'm Lookin' Out the Window/Do You Want to Dance. (2). Columbia DB 4828. May.

It'll Be Me/Since I Lost You. (2). Columbia DB 4886. August.

EPs

Cliff's Hit Parade: I Love You/Theme For a Dream/A Girl Like You/When the Girl in Your Arms. February.

Cliff Richard No. 1: Forty Days/Catch Me/How Wonderful to Know/Tough Enough. April.

Hits from The Young Ones: The Young Ones/Got a Funny Feeling/Lessons in Love/We Say Yeah. May.

Cliff Richard No. 2: Fifty Tears for Every Kiss/The Night Is So Lonely/Poor Boy/Y' Arriva. June.

Cliff's Hits: It'll Be Me/Since I Lost You/Do You Want to Dance/I'm Looking Out the Window. November.

ALBUMS

32 Minutes and 17 Seconds With Cliff Richard: It'll Be Me/So I've Been Told/How Long Is Forever/I'm Walkin' the Blues/Turn Around/Blueberry Hill/Let's Make a Memory/When My Dreamboat Comes Home/I'm On My Way/Spanish Harlem/You Don't Know/Falling in Love With Love/Who Are We to Say/I Wake Up Cryin'. Mono SX 1431, stereo SCX 3436. October.

1963

SINGLES

The Next Time/Bachelor Boy. (1). Columbia DB 4950. February.

Summer Holiday/Dancing Shoes. (1). Columbia DB 4977. February.

Lucky Lips/I Wonder. (4). Columbia DB 7034. May.

It's All in the Game/Your Eyes Tell on You. (2). Columbia DB 7089. August.

Don't Talk to Him/Say You're Mine. (2). Columbia DB 7150. November. Re-entered charts February 1964 (50).

EPs

Time for Cliff and the Shadows: So I've Been Told/I'm Walkin' the Blues/When My Dreamboat Comes Home/Blueberry Hill/You Don't Know. March.

Holiday Carnival: Carnival/Moonlight Bay/Some of These Days/For You, For Me. May.

Hits from Summer Holiday: Summer Holiday/The Next Time/Dancing Shoes/Bachelor Boy. June.

More Hits from Summer Holiday: Seven Days to a Holiday/Stranger in Town/Really Waltzing/All at Once. September.

Cliff's Lucky Lips: It's All in the Game/Your Eyes Tell on You/Lucky Lips/I Wonder. October.

Love Songs: I'm in the Mood For You/Secret Love/Love Letters/I Only Have Eyes For You. November.

ALBUMS

Summer Holiday: Seven Days to a Holiday/Summer Holiday/Let Us Take You For a Ride/Les Girls/Round and Round/Foot Tapper/Stranger in Town/Orlando's Mime/Bachelor Boy/A Swingin' Affair/Really Waltzing/All at Once/Dancing Shoes/Jugoslav Wedding/The Next Time/Big News. Mono SX 1472, stereo SCX 3462. January.

Cliff's Hit Album: Move It/Living Doll/Travellin' Light/A Voice in the Wilderness/Fall in Love With You/Please Don't Tease/Nine Times Out of Ten/I Love You/Theme For a Dream/A Girl Like You/When the Girl in Your Arms Is the Girl in Your Heart/The Young Ones/I'm Looking Out the Window/Do You Want to Dance. Mono SX 1512, stereo SCX 1512. July.

When in Spain: Perfidia/Amor Amor Amor/Frenesi/You Belong to My Heart/Vaya Con Dios/Sweet and Gentle/Maria No Mas/Kiss/Perhaps Perhaps Perhaps/Magic Is the Moonlight/Carnival/Sway. Mono SX 1541, stereo SCX 3488. September.

1964

SINGLES

I'm the Lonely One/Watch What You Do With My Baby. (8). Columbia DB 7203. January.

Constantly/True True Lovin'. (4). Columbia DB 7272. April.

On the Beach/A Matter of Moments. (7). Columbia DB 7305. June.

The Twelfth of Never/I'm Afraid to Go Home. (8). Columbia DB 7372. October.

I Could Easily Fall in Love With You/I'm in Love With You. (9). Columbia DB 7420. December.

EPs

When in France: La Mer/Boum/
J'attendrai/C'est si bon. February.
Cliff Sings Don't Talk to Him: Don't Talk
to Him/Say You're Mine/Spanish
Harlem/Who Are We to Say/Falling
in Love With Love. March.
Cliff's Palladium Successes: I'm the Lonely
One/Watch What You Do With My
Baby/Perhaps Perhaps Perhaps/
Frenesi. May.
Wonderful Life: Wonderful Life/Do You
Remember/What've I Gotta Do/
Walkin'. August.
A Forever Kind of Love: A Forever Kind of
Love/It's Wonderful to Be Young/
Constantly/True True Lovin'.
September.
Wonderful Life No. 2: A Matter of
Moments/Girl in Every Port/A Little
Imagination/In the Stars. October.
Hits from Wonderful Life: On the Beach/
We Love a Movie/Home/All Kinds
of People. December.

ALBUMS

Wonderful Life: Wonderful Life/A Girl in
Every Port/Walkin'/A Little
Imagination/Home/On the Beach/In
the Stars/We Love a Movie/Do You
Remember/What've I Gotta Do/
Theme for Young Lovers/All Kinds
of People/A Matter of Moments/
Youth and Experience. Mono SX
1628, stereo, SCX 3515. July.
Aladdin and His Wonderful Lamp: Emperor
Theme/Chinese Street Scene/Me Oh
My/I Could Easily Fall in Love With
You/There's Gotta Be a Way/Ballet
(Rubies, Emeralds, Sapphires,
Diamonds)/Dance of the Warriors/
Friends/Dragon Dance/Genie With
the Light Brown Lamp/Make Ev'ry
Day a Carnival/Widow Twankey's
Song/I'm Feeling Oh So Lovely/I've
Said Too Many Things/Evening
Comes/Havin' Fun. Mono SX 1676,
stereo SCX 3522. December.

1965

SINGLES

The Minute You're Gone/Just Another
Guy. (1). Columbia DB 7496. March.
Angel/Razzle Dazzle (export single).
Columbia DC 762. May.
On My Word/Just a Little Bit Too Late.
(12). Columbia DB 7596. June.
The Time in Between/Look Before You
Love. (22). Columbia DB 7660.
August.
Wind Me Up (Let Me Go)/The Night.
(2). Columbia DB 7745. November.

EPs

Why Don't They Understand: Why Don't
They Understand/Where the Four
Winds Blow/The Twelfth of Never/
I'm Afraid to Go Home. February.
*Cliff's Hits from Aladdin and His Wonderful
Lamp:* Havin' Fun/Evening Comes/
Friends/I Could Easily Fall in Love
With You. March.
Look in My Eyes Maria: Look in My Eyes
Maria/Where Is Your Heart/Maria/
If I Give My Heart to You. May.
Angel: Angel/I Only Came to Say
Goodbye/On My Word/The Minute
You're Gone. September.
Take Four: Boom Boom/My Heart Is an
Open Book/Lies and Kisses/Sweet
and Gentle. October.

ALBUMS

Cliff Richard: Angel Sway/I Only Came
to Say Goodbye/Take Special Care/
Magic Is the Moonlight/House
Without Windows/Razzle Dazzle/I
Don't Wanna Love You/It's Not For
Me to Say/You Belong to My Heart/
Again/Perfidia/Kiss/Reelin' and
Rockin'. Mono SX 1709, stereo SCX
3456. April.
More Hits – By Cliff: It'll be Me/The
Next Time/Bachelor Boy/Summer
Holiday/Dancing Shoes/Lucky Lips/
It's All in the Game/Don't Talk to
Him/I'm the Lonely One/
Constantly/On the Beach/A Matter
of Moments/The Twelfth of Never/I
Could Easily Fall in Love With You.
Mono SX 1737, stereo SCX 3555.
July.
When in Rome: Come Prima/Volare/
Autumn Concerta/The Questions/
Maria's Her Name/Don't Talk to
Him/Just Say I Love Her/Arrivederci
Roma/Carina/A Little Grain of
Sand/House Without Windows/Che
Cosa Del Farai Mio Amore/Tell Me
You're Mine. Mono SX 1762, no
stereo version. August.
Love is Forever: Everybody Needs
Someone to Love/Long Ago and Far
Away/All of a Sudden My Heart
Sings/Have I Told You Lately That I
Love You/Fly Me to the Moon/A
Summer Place/I Found a Rose/My
Foolish Heart/Through the Eye of a
Needle/My Colouring Book/I Walk
Alone/Someday You'll Want Me to
Want You/Paradise Lost/Look
Homeward Angel. Mono SX 1769,
stereo SCX 3569. November.

1966

SINGLES

Blue Turns to Grey/Somebody Loses.
(15). Columbia DB 7866. March.
Visions/What Would I Do (For the Love
of a Girl). (7). Columbia DB 8968.
July.
Time Drags By/La La La Song. (10).
Columbia DB 8017. October.
In the Country/Finders Keepers. (6).
Columbia DB 8094. December.

EPs

Wind Me Up: Wind Me Up/In the
Night/The Time in Between/Look
Before You Love. February.
Hits from When in Rome: Come Prima
(The First Time)/Nel Blu Dipinto, Di
Blu (Volare)/Dicitencello Vuie (Just
Say I Love Her)/Arrivederci Roma.
April.
Love Is Forever: My Colouring Book/Fly
Me to the Moon/ Someday/
Everybody Needs Somebody to Love.
June.
La La La La La: La La La La La/
Solitary Man/Things We Said
Today/Never Knew What Love
Could Do. December.

ALBUMS

Kinda Latin: Blame It on the Bossa
Nova/Blowing in the Wind/Quiet
Night of Quiet Stars/Eso Beso/The
Girl from Ipanema/One Note
Samba/Fly Me to the Moon/Our
Day Will Come/Quando Quando
Quando/Come Closer to Me/
Meditation/Concrete and Clay.
Mono SX 6039, stereo SCX 6039.
May.
Finders Keepers: Finders Keepers/Time
Drags By/Washerwoman/La La La
Song/My Way/Senorita/Spanish
Music-Fiesta/This Day/Paella/
Medley (Finders Keepers/My Way/
Paella/Fiesta)/Run to the Door/
Where Did the Summer Go/Into
Each Life/Some Rain Must Fall.
Mono SX 6079. December.

1967

SINGLES

It's All Over/Why Wasn't I Born Rich.
(9). Columbia DB 8150. March.
I'll Come Running/I Get the Feelin'.
(26). Columbia DB 8210. June.
The Day I Met Marie/Our Story Book.
(10). Columbia DB 8245. August.
All My Love/Sweet Little Jesus Boy. (6).
Columbia DB 8293. November.

EPs

Cinderella: Come Sunday/Peace and
Quiet/She Needs Him More Than
Me/Hey Doctor Man. May.
Carol Singers: God Rest You Merry,
Gentlemen/In the Bleak Midwinter/
Unto Us a Boy Is Born/While
Shepherds Watched/O Little Town
of Bethlehem. November.

ALBUMS

Cinderella: Welcome to Stonybroke/Why Wasn't I Born Rich/Peace and Quiet/The Flyder and the Spy/Poverty/The Hunt/In the Country/Come Sunday/Dare I Love Him Like I Do (Jackie Lee)/If Our Dreams Came True/Autumn/The King's Place/She Needs Him More than Me/Hey Doctor Man. Mono SX 6103, stereo SCX 6103. January.

Don't Stop Me Now: Shout/One Fine Day/I'll Be Back/Heartbeat/I Saw Her Standing There/Hang On to a Dream/You Gotta Tell Me/Homeward Bound/Good Golly Miss Molly/Don't Make Promises/Move It/Don't/Dizzy Miss Lizzy/Baby It's You/My Babe/Save the Last Dance For Me. Mono SX 6133, stereo SCX 6133. April.

Good News: Good News/It Is No Secret/We Shall Be Changed/Twenty-Third Psalm/Go Where I Send Thee/What a Friend We Have in Jesus/All Glory Laud and Honour/Just a Closer Walk With Thee/The King of Love My Shepherd Is/Mary What You Gonna Name That Pretty Little Baby/When I Survey the Wondrous Cross/Take My Hand Precious Lord/Get on Board Little Children/May the Good Lord Bless and Keep You. Mono SX 6167, stereo SCX 6167. October.

1968

SINGLES

Congratulations/High and Dry. (1). Columbia DB 8376. March.

I'll Love You Forever Today/Girl You'll Be a Woman Soon. (27). Columbia DB 8437. June.

Marianne/Mr Nice. (22). Columbia DB 8476. September.

Don't Forget to Catch Me/What's More (I Don't Need Her). (21). Columbia DB 8503. November.

ALBUMS

Cliff in Japan: Shout/I'll Come Runnin'/The Minute You're Gone/On the Beach/Hang On to a Dream/Spanish Harlem/Finders Keepers/Visions/Move It/Living Doll/La La La La La/Twist and Shout/Evergreen Tree/What I'd Say/Dynamite/Medley (Let's Make a Memory/The Young Ones/Lucky Lips/Summer Holiday/We Say Yeah). Mono SX 6244, stereo SCX 6244. May.

Two a Penny: Two a Penny/I'll Love You Forever Today/Questions/Long Is the Night (instrumental)/Lonely Girl/And Me (I'm on the Outside Now)/Daybreak/Twist and Shout/Celeste (instrumental)/Wake Up Wake Up/Cloudy/Red Rubber Ball/Close to Kathy/Rattler. Mono SX 6262, stereo SCX 6262. August.

Established 1958: Don't Forget to Catch Me/Voyage to the Bottom of the Bath (The Shadows)/Not the Way That It Should Be/Poem (The Shadows)/The Dreams I Dream/The Average Life of a Daily Man (The Shadows)/Somewhere By the Sea/Banana Man (The Shadows)/Girl On the Bus/The Magical Mrs Clamps (The Shadows)/Ooh La La/Here I Go Again Loving You (The Shadows)/What's Behind the Eyes of Mary/Maggie's Samba (The Shadows). Mono SX 6282, stereo SCX 6282. September.

1969

SINGLES

Good Times/Occasional Rain. (12). Columbia DB 8548. February.

Big Ship/She's Leaving You. (8). Columbia DB 8581. May.

Throw Down a Line/Reflections (with Hank Marvin). (7). Columbia DB 8615. September.

With the Eyes of a Child/So Long. (20). Columbia DB 8641. December.

ALBUMS

The Best of Cliff: The Minute You're Gone/Congratulations/Girl You'll Be a Woman Soon/The Time in Between/Time Drags By/In the Country/Blue Turns to Grey/On My Word/Wind Me Up/Visions/It's All Over/I'll Come Runnin'/The Day I Met Marie/All My Love. Mono SX 6343, stereo SCX 6343. June.

Sincerely Cliff: Sam/London's Not Too Far/Take Action/I'm Not Getting Married/In the Past/Always/Will You Love Me Tomorrow/You'll Want Me/Time/For Emily Whenever I May Find Her/Baby I Could Be So Good at Loving You/Take Good Care of Her/When I Find You/Punch and Judy. Mono SX 6357, stereo SCX 6357. October.

1970

SINGLES

Joy of Living/Boogatoo, Leave My Woman Alone. (25). Columbia DB 8687. February.

Goodbye Sam, Hello Samantha/You Never Can Tell. (6). Columbia DB 8685. June.

Ain't Got Time Anymore/Monday Comes Too Soon. (21). Columbia DB 8708. September.

ALBUMS

Cliff 'Live' at The Talk of the Town: Intro (Congratulations)/Shout/All My Love/Ain't Nothing But a House-Party/Something Good/If Ever I Should Leave You/Girl You'll Be a Woman Soon/Hank's Medley/London's Not Too Far/The Dreams I Dream/The Day I Met Marie/La La La La La/A Taste of Honey (guitar solo)/The Lady Came from Baltimore/When I'm Sixty-Four/What's More (I Don't Need Her)/Bows and Fanfare/Congratulations/Visions/Finale (Congratulations). Regal SRS 5031. July.

About That Man: Sweet Little Jesus Boy/Where Is That Man/Can It Be True/Reflections/Cliff tells the story of Jesus in the words of the Living Bible. SCX 6408. October.

Tracks 'n' Grooves: Early in the Morning/As I Walk Into the Morning of Your Life/Love, Truth and Emily Stone/My Head Goes Around/Put My Mind at Ease/Abraham Martin and John/The Girl Can't Help It/Bang Bang My Baby Shot Me Down/I'll Make It Up to You/I'd Just Be Fool Enough/Don't Let Tonight Ever End/What a Silly Thing to Do/Your Heart's Not in Your Love/Don't Ask Me to Be Friends/Are You Only Fooling Me. SCX 6435. November.

His Land: Ezekiel's Vision (Ralph Carmichael Orchestra)/Dry Bones (Ralph Carmichael Orchestra)/His Land/Jerusalem, Jerusalem/The New Twenty-Third/His Land/Hava Nagila (Ralph Carmichael Orchestra)/Over in Bethlehem (and Cliff Barrows)/Keep Me Where Love Is/He's Everything to Me (and Cliff Barrows)/Narration and Hallelujah Chorus (Cliff Barrows). SCX 6443. November.

1971

SINGLES

Sunny Honey Girl/Don't Move Away (with Olivia Newton-John)/I Was Only Fooling Myself. (19). Columbia DB 8747. January.

Silvery Rain/Annabella Umbarella/Time Flies. (27). Columbia DB 8774. April.

Flying Machine/Pigeon. (37). Columbia DB 8797. July.

Sing a Song of Freedom/A Thousand Conversations. (13). Columbia DB 8836. November.

1972

SINGLES

Jesus/Mr Cloud. (35). Columbia DB 8864. March.

Living in Harmony/Empty Chairs. (12). Columbia DB 8917. August.

Brand New Song/The Old Accordion. (No chart placing). Columbia DB 8957. November.

ALBUMS

The Best of Cliff Volume 2: Goodbye Sam, Hello Samantha/Marianne/Throw Down a Line/Jesus/Sunny Honey Girl/I Ain't Got Time Anymore/Flying Machine/Sing a Song of Freedom/With the Eyes of a Child/Good Times (Better Times)/I'll Love You Forever Today/The Joy of Living/Silvery Rain/Big Ship. SCX 6519. November.

1973

SINGLES

Power to All Our Friends/Come Back Billie Joe (4). EMI 2012. March.

Help It Along/Tomorrow Rising/The Days of Love/Ashes to Ashes. (29). EMI 2022. May.

Take Me High/Celestial Houses. (27). EMI 2088. December.

ALBUMS

Take Me High: It's Only Money/Midnight Blue/Hover (instrumental)/Why (and Anthony Andrews)/Life/Driving/The Game/Brumburger Duet (and Debbie Watling)/Take Me High/The Anti-Brotherhood of Man/Winning/Driving (instrumental)/Join the Band/The World Is Love/Brumburger (finale). EMI EMC 3016. December.

1974

SINGLES

(You Keep Me) Hanging On/Love Is Here. (13). EMI 2150. May.

ALBUMS

Help It Along: Day by Day/Celestial Houses/Jesus/Silvery Rain/Jesus Loves You/Fire and Rain/Yesterday, Today, Forever/Help It Along/Amazing Grace/Higher Ground/Sing a Song of Freedom. EMI EMA 768. June.

The 31st of February Street: 31st of February Street/Give Me Back That Old Familiar Feeling/The Leaving/Travellin' Light/There You Go Again/Nothing to Remind Me/Our Love Could Be So Real/No Matter What/Fireside Song/Going Away/Long Long Time/You Will Never Know/The Singer/31st of February Street Closing. EMI EMC 3048. November.

1975

SINGLES

It's Only Me You've Left Behind/You're the One. (No chart placing). EMI 2279. March.

Honky-Tonk Angel/Wouldn't You Know It. (No chart placing). EMI 2344. September.

1976

SINGLES

Miss You Nights/Love Is Enough. (15). EMI 2376. February.

Devil Woman/Love On. (9). EMI 2485. May.

I Can't Ask for Anything More Than You Babe/Junior Cowboy. (17). EMI 2499. August.

Hey Mr Dream Maker/No One Waits. (31). EMI 2559. December.

ALBUMS

I'm Nearly Famous: I Can't Ask for Anymore Than You/It's No Use Pretending/I'm Nearly Famous/Lovers/Junior Cowboy/Miss You Nights/I Wish You'd Change Your Mind/Devil Woman/Such Is the Mystery/You've Got to Give Me All Your Lovin'/If You Walked Away/Alright, It's Alright. EMI EMC 3122. May. Reissued May 1982.

1977

SINGLES

My Kinda Life/Nothing Left for Me to Say. (15). EMI 2584. March.

When Two Worlds Drift Apart/That's Why I Love You. (46). EMI 2663. June.

ALBUMS

Every Face Tells a Story: My Kinda Life/Must Be Love/When Two Worlds Drift Apart/You Got Me Wondering/Every Face Tells a Story (It Never Tells a Lie)/Try a Smile/Hey Mr Dream Maker/Give Me Love Your Way/Up In the World/Don't Turn the Light Out/It'll Be Me Babe/Spider Man. EMI EMC 3172. March.

Cliff Richard's 40 Golden Greats: Move It/Living Doll/Travellin' Light/Fall in Love With You/Please Don't Tease/Nine Times Out of Ten/Theme for a Dream/Gee Whizz It's You/When the Girl in YourArms Is the Girl in Your Heart/A Girl Like You/The Young Ones/Do You Want to Dance/I'm Lookin' Out the Window/It'll Be Me/Bachelor Boy/The Next Time/Summer Holiday/Lucky Lips/It's All in the Game/Don't Talk to Him/Constantly/On the Beach/I Could Easily Fall in Love With You/The Minute You're Gone/Wind Me Up (Let Me Go)/Visions/Blue Turns to Grey/In the Country/The Day I Met Marie/All My Love/Congratulations/Throw Down a Line/Goodbye Sam, Hello Samantha/Sing a Song of Freedom/Power to All Our Friends/(You Keep Me) Hangin' On/Miss You Nights/Devil Woman/I Can't Ask for Anything More Than You/My Kinda Life. EMI EMTVS 6. October.

Small Corners: Why Should the Devil Have All the Good Music/I Love/I've Got News For You/Hey Watcha Say/I Wish We'd All Been Ready/Joseph/Good on the Sally Army/Goin' Home/Up in Canada/Yes He Lives/When I Survey the Wondrous Cross. EMI EMC 3219. November.

1978

SINGLES

Yes He Lives/Good on the Sally Army. (No chart placing). EMI 2730. January.

Please Remember Me/Please Don't Tease. (No chart placing). EMI 2832. July.

Can't Take the Hurt Anymore/Needing a Friend. (No chart placing). EMI 2885. November.

ALBUMS

Green Light: Green Light/Under Lock and Key/She's a Gipsy/Count Me Out/Please Remember Me/Never Even Thought/Free My Soul/Start All Over Again/While She's Young/Can't Take the Hurt Anymore/Ease Along. EMI EMC 3231. October.

1979

SINGLES

Green Light/Imagine Love. (57). EMI 2920. March.

We Don't Talk Anymore/Count Me Out. (1). EMI 2975. July.

Hot Shot/Walking in the Light. (46). EMI 5003. November.

ALBUMS

Thank You Very Much (with The Shadows): The Young Ones/Do You Want to Dance/The Day I Met Marie/Shadoogie (The Shadows)/Atlantis (The Shadows)/Nivram (The Shadows)/Apache (The Shadows)/Please Don't Tease/Miss You Nights/Move It/Willie and the Hand Jive/All Shook Up/Devil Woman/Why Should the Devil Have All the Good Music/End of the Show (Cliff plus Shadows). EMI EMTV 15. February.

Rock 'n' Roll Juvenile: Monday Thru' Friday/Doing Fine/Cities May Fall/You Know That I Love You/My Luck Won't Change/Rock 'n' Roll Juvenile/Sci-Fi/Fallin' in Love/Carrie/Hot Shot/Language of Love/We Don't Talk Anymore. EMI EMC 3307. September.

1980

SINGLES

Carrie/Moving In. (4). EMI 5006. February.

Dreamin'/Dynamite. (8). EMI 5095. August.

Suddenly (with Olivia Newton-John)/You Made Me Love You (Newton-John only). (15). Jet 7002. October.

ALBUMS

Cliff – The Early Years (this album was scheduled for release February 1980 but its release was cancelled): Please Don't Tease/Willie and the Hand Jive/'D' in Love/High Class Baby/Mean Woman Blues/Nine Times Out of Ten/My Feet Hit the Ground/Apron Strings/Livin' Lovin' Doll/Never Mind/Schoolboy Crush/It'll Be Me/Gee Whizz It's You/Choppin' 'n' Changin'/Blue Suede Shoes/Dynamite/Mean Streak/She's Gone/I Cannot Find a True Love/Move It.

I'm No Hero: Take Another Look/Anything I Can Do/A Little in Love/Here (So Doggone Blue)/Give a Little Bit More/In the Night/I'm No Hero/Dreamin'/A Heart Will Break/Everyman. EMI EMA 796. August.

1981

SINGLES

A Little in Love/Keep on Looking. (15). EMI 5123. February.

Wired For Sound/Hold On. (4). EMI 5221. August.

Daddy's Home/Shakin' All Over. (2). EMI 5251. November.

ALBUMS

Cliff – Love Songs: Miss You Nights/Constantly/Up In the World/Carrie/A Voice in the Wilderness/The Twelfth of Never/I Could Easily Fall/The Day I Met Marie/Can't Take the Hurt Anymore/A Little in Love/The Minute You're Gone/Visions/When Two Worlds Drift Apart/The Next Time/It's All in the Game/Don't Talk to Him/When the Girl in Your Arms/Theme for a Dream/Fall in Love With You/We Don't Talk Anymore. EMTV 27. June.

Wired for Sound: Wired for Sound/Once in a While/Better Than I Know Myself/Oh No Don't Let Go/'Cos I Love That Rock 'n' Roll/Broken Doll/Lost in a Lonely World/Summer Rain/Young Love/Say You Don't Mind/Daddy's Home. EMI EMC 3377. September.

1982

SINGLES

The Only Way/Under the Influence. (10). EMI 5138. July.

Where Do We Go From Here/Discovering. (60). EMI 5341. September.

Little Town/Love and a Helping Hand/You, Me and Jesus. (11). EMI 5348. November.

Oldies reissued in February, available separately or in a special boxed set:

Move It/Schoolboy Crush. (-). DB 4178.

Living Doll/Apron Strings. (-). DB 4306.

Travellin' Light/Dynamite. (-). DB 4351.

Please Don't Tease/Where Is My Heart. (-). DB 4479.

The Young Ones/We Say Yeah. (-). DB 4761.

The Next Time/Bachelor Boy. (-). DB 4950.

Summer Holiday/Dancing Shoes. (-). DB 4977.

Wind Me Up (Let Me Go)/The Night. (-). DB 7745.

Congratulations/High and Dry. (-). DB 8376.

Miss You Nights/Love Is Enough. (-). DB 2376.

Devil Woman/Love On, Shine On. (-). EMI 2458.

We Don't Talk Anymore/Count Me Out. (-). EMI 2975. (This was not a reissue since it was not deleted, but it is included in the boxed set.)

ALBUMS

Now You See Me, Now You Don't: The Only Way Out/First Date/Thief in the Night/Where Do We Go From Here/Son of Thunder/Little Town/It Has to Be You, It Has to Be Me/The Water Is Wide/Now You See Me, Now You Don't/Be in My Heart/Discovering. EMI EMC 3415. August.

1983

SINGLES

She Means Nothing to Me (with Phil Everly)/Man and a Woman (Phil Everly). (9). Capitol CL 276. February.

True Love Ways/Galadriel. EMI 5385. April.

ALBUMS

Dressed for the Occasion (recorded at a charity concert at the Royal Albert Hall, London, November 1982) Green Light/We Don't Talk Anymore/True Love Ways/Softly As I Leave You/Carrie/Miss You Nights/Galadriel/Maybe Some Day/Thief in the Night/Up in the World/Treasure of Love/Devil Woman. EMI EMC 3432.

INDEX